How to Find and MARRY the PERSON God Has for You

By Victoria K. Fuller

Published by Ada Publishers
P.O. Drawer 1928
Wheaton, Maryland 20915-1928
U.S.A.

ISBN 0-9636891-6-9
Library of Congress Catalog Card Number 93-71770

Dedication

To my mother, Anne
who prayed for many years
that God would send me the right man

and

My sister-in-law, Grace
who made it possible for Ben to attend college in the U.S.
Had she not done so, Ben and I might never have met.

Acknowledgements

I am very much indebted to several people for their guidance and help in the preparation of this book. My husband, Ben provided so much valuable assistance in writing the manuscript that this book is really a joint effort. Special thanks to Jerry, Johnny, and Janice, all very busy people, who took time to read the manuscript and offer helpful suggestions and encouragement.

Mary Abrams, a gifted professional writer and editor, helped me clarify my message to singles. I sincerely appreciate her thorough and thoughtful editing of the book.

To my loving children, Joshua and Kayte, a special "thank you" for giving Mommy undistracted time to work on this project.

Finally, I would like to thank the many friends who generously allowed me to share their experiences. Their stories put a human face on the ideas in this book, providing practical illustrations of the trials and triumphs so many people experience in their search for happiness, and ultimately demonstrating the beauty and validity of God's Word.

How to Find and MARRY the PERSON God Has for You

Contents

Chapter One

Take the Critical First Step

"Oh that I might have my request; and that God would grant me the thing I long for" (Job 6:8, KJV).

Much is written about good Christians who find contentment, happiness, peace, and fulfilling ministries as single people. Many people who may not have been called to celibacy learn to live in the single state and feel no pressing need to pursue marriage. If you are one of these, I thank the Lord for you and pray that His grace will continue to sustain you.

Experience shows, however, that many single Christians want desperately to be married. And although Job, in the quotation cited above, was praying for death as a way out of his misery, many single people can relate to the strong feelings he expressed in his prayer. If you are crying out to the Lord, praying that your quest for a lifetime partner will be granted, don't despair. Your answer may be closer and better than you believe possible, because God promises to give us exceedingly, abundantly, above all we can think or imagine.

My Story

Several years ago, I found myself with an overwhelming desire to be married. Like many single people, I received a lot of well-meaning advice. Friends counselled me to seek contentment as a single woman, and not to make marriage a priority for my life. Somehow, try as I might, I could never accept that advice. I did not just want to find someone to love. I wished desperately for a husband, children, and a family of my own. Prayer, counselling, and Bible study helped me turn

1

that obsession into a positive priority, and God answered my prayers. Today, I'm married to a wonderful Christian man--the man of my prayers--and we have two beautiful children.

God is no respecter of persons. If he did it for me, He'll do it for you.

What I learned is that it is not enough just to *want*. You must have a *fervent desire* to be married. As long as you are willing to tolerate being single, so you will remain. It is not a paradox to live contentedly as a single person and still want fervently to be married. The many human stories in this book--all true--will demonstrate that those two conditions are not mutually exclusive.

As a single Christian, I was actively involved with church activities and had a satisfying career, many friends, and a close-knit family. Still, I wished desperately to be married. I longed for a husband and children. And as the years went by with no prospect in sight, I became increasingly despondent.

I was happy for friends who had found their mates, and who asked me to be part of their weddings. But while I rejoiced for them, I began to feel like a prime example of the aphorism, "Always a bridesmaid, never the bride." Seeing happy couples and families together made me feel empty inside. I was tired of putting on a smiling face for my married friends when I was really depressed and lonely. I wanted companionship and love. I was tired of coming home from church alone every Sunday; tired of going to dinner with girlfriends; tired of shopping alone. I wanted to find someone waiting for me when I got home from work every evening, someone to hold me in his arms and ask about my day.

I hadn't received any serious attention from a gentleman for so long I'd forgotten what it was like. I didn't really have any male friends; the single men in my church were hesitant to be too friendly, because, as they said, they didn't want to give women the wrong impression or "lead them on." Unless they were in the same ministry, most of the men in my church were careful not to sit next to the same woman two Sundays in a row, for fear they would be linked together.

Sometimes I thought, "Maybe God has forgotten me." I've since learned that my feelings are typical of thousands of Christian single people.

Some become bitter and resentful, giving up any hope of marriage. Others sublimate their feelings by involving themselves in numerous activities. Some compromise their beliefs and marry unbelievers.

One single friend of mine became so disheartened that, at age forty-two, she deliberately conceived a child with an unbeliever. She told friends she knew it was a sin, but wanted a child so desperately that she didn't care. She had begun to feel that God would never answer her prayers.

What is happening in our churches? Why do single people find themselves in these situations? Is there something fundamentally wrong with the advice that well-meaning counsellors are giving single people? The truth is that most such counselling focuses on the importance of seeking contentment in the single state, joining Christian singles clubs, and getting involved in ministry. Rather than helping people establish families of their own, such advice often results in frustration, resentment, compromise, and denial. Too many singles are forced to suppress their natural desire to be married and have families of their own for fear of seeming ungrateful or "unholy."

The Bible admonishes Christians not to lie to one another, but to speak the truth in love. We must learn to be open about our desire to be married. Marriage is the will of God for most Christians, and pursuing the will of God should have a high priority for those who are called to marriage. I know from my own experience that no one can assume marriage will "happen by itself." We must devote to the finding of a mate the same degree of attention, planning, and energy we would devote to any other worthwhile goal.

Allen's Unique Dream

When my husband, Ben, was in his early twenties, working as an accountant in London, he had a very good friend named Allen O'Neal. Allen later went into the ministry as a pastor. When Ben came to the United States, they corresponded for a while, then lost contact.

Some twelve years later, we were pleasantly surprised to run into Allen while visiting a friend's church one Sunday. That day, Allen was the guest preacher. After the service, we invited him to our home and asked him to spend a few days with us before returning to London. Allen told

3

us he had been married for several years to a beautiful lady, Maggie, and that they had one son. We asked him how they had met, and he was happy to tell us.

A few years earlier, he had begun to pray for the Lord's help in finding the right person to marry. One night, he had a vivid dream. He had been invited to preach at a church in a nearby town. He could not identify the church or the town, but while he was waiting to preach, the pastor introduced a radiant young woman who would sing a solo. Allen was instantly attracted by the grace with which she carried herself, and by her angelic voice that seemed to lift the congregation on wings of praise. He knew immediately that this young woman was meant to be his wife. From the moment he saw her in his dream he felt deeply commited, even though they had never met.

When he awoke, the woman's image was imprinted in his mind. He recorded every detail of the dream in his prayer diary, including a vivid description of the young woman. That day he began to pray fervently that he would find her. He decided that if he ever did, he would try to win her love without ever mentioning the dream. As a minister, Allen had seen numerous instances of people telling their mates that "the Lord revealed to me in a dream that you are supposed to be my wife" (or husband), sometimes with disastrous results.

Allen's Answer to Prayer

Almost a year and a half later, Allen was invited to be guest preacher one Sunday morning at a church in a nearby town. Before Allen was to preach, the pastor introduced the guest soloist for the service. And there she was, the radiant young woman Allen had dreamed of nearly a year earlier. Recognizing her, he began to tremble, and felt sweat running down his spine. After the service, Allen asked to meet the soloist who had sung so beautifully, and the pastor introduced him to Maggie. Although he was thrilled by the miracle that seemed to be happening, he tried to contain his excitement.

He knew that this was the woman of his dream, the answer to his prayers. But he maintained his resolve not to tell her about the dream, or to show her the notes in his diary, until she had agreed to marry him. Allen invited Maggie to sing in his church the following Sunday, which she did. At Allen's suggestion, she began attending Bible studies in his church. One Wednesday night, Allen took her aside and said, "Maggie, I have something I want to say to you. I love you and I want you to consider becoming my wife. I believe you will tell me yes, but please go ahead and pray about it." Caught completely off guard, Maggie agreed that she did indeed need time to think and pray. And after several weeks she joyously accepted his proposal.

Maggie told her parents she and Allen wanted to be married. Her father was happy for her, but she was surprised to encounter tremendous resistance from her mother, Ida. Ida vowed that she would see to it that they would never marry--in her own words, "not while I am alive." She did not feel that a pastor could give her daughter an appropriate standard of living. She even threatened to disinherit Maggie if she married Allen.

Maggie and Allen resolved that they would not marry without the full blessing of both of her parents. Despite Ida's strong opposition, Allen knew beyond a shadow of doubt that Maggie was meant to be his wife. For years, he had prayed for someone with all of Maggie's qualities. In Maggie, he had found the manifestation of his dream and the confirmation of his prayers, and he would not surrender to Ida's objections.

Although he saw her as a threat to his "land of promise," he was determined to win her approval. The spiritual battle was launched, pitting Allen's conviction of the rightness of their marriage against her mother's determination to prevent it. He and Maggie began by praying that God would break down Ida's resistance and convince her, of her own free will, to give her blessing to the marriage. In the meantime, Allen had still not told Maggie about his dream.

Winning the Spiritual Battle

Weeks went by, and God began to arrange circumstances to help resolve the problem. Maggie's brother Chris had a very successful business that had suddenly begun to fail. He was encountering all sorts of difficulties; nothing he did seemed to go right. One day, while Allen was in his study, the Lord laid it on his heart that Chris would come to seek counsel from him that evening. God told Allen specific issues Chris would talk about, and the advice he should give in response.

Sure enough, that evening a downcast, forlorn Chris came to Allen's study. He poured his heart out about his business troubles, just as the

5

Lord had revealed that he would. When he finished, Allen responded as God had instructed him, and in the process, was able to lead Chris to the Lord. Chris went home and did exactly as Allen had advised. Within a matter of weeks, Chris' company received a multimillion-dollar contract from a foreign client.

At about the same time, Barbara, one of Maggie's cousins, was expecting a baby. There were complications with the pregnancy, and her doctors were afraid she might lose the child. They recommended that she be confined to bed for the remainder of the pregnancy. Maggie told Allen about Barbara's situation, and they went to her house to pray for her. Barbara's situation improved dramatically. She went on to have an uneventful pregnancy, and delivered a beautiful baby boy a few months later. The family was ecstatic, and the proud parents named the child Allen. That experience also led Ted, Barbara's husband, to the Lord.

Hearing about Allen's successful counselling with Chris, and the miracle God had worked for Ted and Barbara, other members of Maggie's family began to seek Allen's counsel. Several began to attend his church. The whole family, except for Ida, became enthusiastic about Allen's and Maggie's engagement. Then something happened that affected Ida directly. Several years earlier, she had been involved in an accident and had required extensive surgery. Since that time, she had frequently experienced stabbing pains in her back and legs. One rainy morning, on her way to the store, she fell and was rushed to the hospital.

She was in severe pain when Maggie and Allen arrived at the hospital to see her. Allen asked Ida if she would allow him to pray for her. Reluctantly, she agreed. Allen anointed her with oil, laid his hands on her forehead and prayed for her. As Ida related later, she felt a surge of power throughout her body when Allen's cool hands touched her forehead. Within a matter of days, Ida left the hospital. Since then, she has never been troubled by the pain that had plagued her for years. After that experience, her opposition to Allen softened.

By that time, the spiritual battle had lasted almost a year and half. Ida finally gave her blessing to Allen and Maggie. She later confessed that her initial opposition was based on her involvement in witchcraft, astrology and other occult practices. As she relates it, the first time she saw Allen, she developed a strong aversion for him, for no apparent reason.

She resolved then and there to do whatever was necessary to prevent his marriage to Maggie.

At the time we got reacquainted with Allen, he and Maggie had been married for about six years. They have a wonderful ministry, a thriving church, and loving relationship with both sets of parents.

Most single people would love to be in Allen's position, with God sending them a clear vision of the person they are supposed to marry. That knowledge would make their lives a lot easier, allowing them to focus and pray specifically and earnestly for their mates. And indeed, the Lord may choose to reveal your mate to you in this fashion. One thing is certain: God treats each one of us uniquely. As the Lord of the universe, He will never run out of different ways to accomplish His purposes, and to reveal his intentions for our lives. So while God answered Allen's prayer for a mate, and even gave him a specific face to hold in his mind, most singles will not receive such a strong message. They will have to start with God's promise alone in their hearts.

Greg's and Kathleen's Story

While I was a junior in college, my brother Gregory enrolled as a freshman at the same university. During his sophomore year, Greg met Kathleen, a bright, attractive, serious-minded young lady. They became very good friends, started dating, and eventually lived together for two semesters. Their love grew, and they made plans to get married.

One evening Greg found a Christian tract on the windshield of his car. He put it in his pocket and read it when he got back to his apartment. Greg said he felt as though the words were written directly and specifically to him. Although ours was a "religious" family, and Greg had gone to church regularly, he had never truly committed his life to the Lord. After reading the tract, however, he felt such strong conviction in his spirit that he went to his bedroom, knelt down and invited Jesus into his life.

When Kathleen came home, Gregory excitedly told her what had happened to him. Because of his religious upbringing, he realized that they could no longer live together before marriage and would have to abstain from sexual relations. Greg's life changed radically. He gave up old habits like drinking and using drugs and tried to convince Kathleen to stop smoking.

Kathleen was totally bewildered by Greg's "good news." She had always felt that she too was a Christian. Now it seemed that Greg and his new-found religion were judging her unfairly. She felt threatened that somehow Greg's new relationship with the Lord had destroyed their own relationship. Deeply hurt, she suggested he must have become "gay," since he no longer desired a sexual relationship.

Although Greg really loved Kathleen, he stood his ground. He told me later that for three weeks, he was confused and frightened. He likened himself to Daniel, who spent twenty-one days struggling with Satan. He had to endure strong opposition from Kathleen, friends, co-workers, and even his own flesh. I invited Greg to come with me to church--the first time since he had been saved. Amazingly, the sermon focused on Daniel, the very same text from scripture that he had been thinking about. This further confirmed for Greg the rightness of his decision to follow the Lord.

Greg called me often during this period, pouring his heart out. Although he loved the Lord and was happy to be saved, he was heart-broken to think he had lost Kathleen and their plans for a life together. We prayed together and I encouraged him to seek counsel from my pastor. One day, Greg asked Kathleen to go with him for counselling about their situation. During the counseling session, the pastor looked Kathleen in the eye and said, "Young lady, if you want to marry Greg, you're going to have to get saved first."

Kathleen remained calm and respectful, but she told Greg later that she was furious at the way the pastor had spoken to her. Even Greg told me that he felt the pastor might have spoken too forcefully. But Greg maintained his ground, and their relationship went into a holding pattern. Later that year, Kathleen began to think seriously about her life. She realized that she had been a Christian in name only. She also saw that the changes in Greg were genuine and lasting, and that God had made a difference in his life.

Soon Kathleen truly committed her life to the Lord and together she and Greg started attending my church. They came to an agreement with the

Lord and decided to follow His primary basis for marriage, which is spiritual compatibility. Finally, after several premarital counseling sessions with our pastor, Greg and Kathleen were married. They have been happily married for twelve years.

Your Relationship with the Lord

The advice in this book is based entirely on the Word of God, dedicated primarily to Christian singles. The Bible says in *Amos 3:3 (KJV)* "can two walk together, except they be agreed?" I believe strongly that you, the reader, and I must be in agreement as we walk together through the pages of this book. Even more importantly, you, and the Lord, and the mate you will choose for marriage must walk in harmony and agreement. Like Greg and Kathleen, you must commit your life to God and become a born-again believer in the Lord Jesus Christ. A personal relationship with the Lord is imperative in order for Him to hear and answer your prayers.

How to Be Saved

> The Bible says, in *Romans 3:23,* that "...all have sinned, and fall short of the glory of God."

If you have never turned over the control of your life to the Lord, the next few pages are written particularly for you. In them, I will try to clarify the message of God's salvation through Jesus, and provide you with information on how to commit your life to the Lord. This is the **first critical step** you must take. After you have done this, you will be ready to receive all that God has for you. God is righteous and desires us to be in a righteous relationship with Him. Since He is righteous and we are not, and cannot of our own strength please Him, He has provided a way for us to meet His righteous requirement. The Bible says in *Hebrews 9:22* that "... without the shedding of blood there is no forgiveness." The Lord Jesus Christ provided the innocent, righteous atoning blood through which we can come into a relationship with God.

We are therefore required to come to God by faith in the finished work of Jesus on the cross of Calvary. On the cross, Jesus took upon Himself all the sins you have committed and will ever commit, and the punishment for them. He took your place on the cross. But the only way to make that substitution effective is for you to accept the fact of what Jesus has done for you. In God's eyes, the work of Jesus on the cross is not effective until you accept it personally and appropriate it for yourself.

How then do you accept and appropriate for yourself the substitionary death of Jesus? The Bible says it must be done by faith. *John 3:16* reads, "For God so loved the world that he gave his one and only Son, that whoever believes in him shall not perish but have eternal life." Your salvation is in believing that God sent Jesus to die for you. Just as you believe promises that people make to you, so you must believe that God is showing you the only way for salvation.

If You Have Never Invited the Lord into Your Life:

The process for believing and confessing the truth of God for the salvation of any individual is clearly outlined in *Romans 10.*

1.   Read *Romans 10:9,10,13*

"If you confess with your mouth, Jesus is Lord, and believe in your heart that God hath raised him from the dead, you will be saved. For it is with your heart that you believe and are justified, and it is with your mouth that you confess and are saved. Everyone who calls on the name of the Lord will be saved."

2.   Pray the sinner's prayer.

On the basis of *Romans 10,* say this prayer aloud:

> *Dear God,*
> *I know from Your Word that I am a sinner, because I have gone my way in rebellion and done things my own way. I also know from Your Word that the consequence of this rebellion is eternal death, eternal separation from Your presence. I thank You that You love me so much that You have made provision to take away this punishment if only I will believe in and agree with you.*
>
> *Thank You for sending the Lord Jesus Christ for my redemption. I believe that Jesus died and took the eternal punishment for my sins on the cross, and was buried, but*

You raised Him from the dead in order to give me eternal life. I repent of all my sins and ask for Your forgiveness. I receive all that Jesus did for me.

Lord Jesus, I invite You to come into my heart and be my Lord and Saviour. Give me the power to live for You. From this day forward, guide me, teach me, direct me to lead a life that will be totally pleasing to You.

Thank You for saving me. Amen

3. You're saved!

If you have prayed this prayer, and believed in your heart, then according to scripture, you are saved. God explains what He has done in your life and where you now stand with Him in *Ezekiel 11:19-20:* "I will give them an undivided heart and put a new spirit in them; I will remove from them their heart of stone and give them a heart of flesh. Then they will follow my decrees and be careful to keep my laws. They will be my people, and I will be their God."

Being saved, then, simply means that you have allowed the Holy Spirit of God to remake and renew your spirit. This spiritual surgery has removed any enmity between your spirit and the Holy Spirit of God. You will become aware of the presence of God and can know and, to a greater measure understand, what He is doing in your life. God has given you a new nature that is in tune with His Holy Spirit.

As it says in *2 Corinthians 5:17 (KJV)*, "Therefore if any man be in Christ, he is a new creature: old things are passed away; behold, all things are become new." God is saying to you, no matter how you were born, your family history, no matter what has happened in your life or what you have done, no matter what your past, behold! Here is the new spiritual you!

Before you invited Christ into your heart, you might have compared your life to a junkyard strewn with scraps and discards--practically unusable material. By inviting Christ into your life, you have allowed God to gather the materials from your junkyard and create a masterpiece that He Himself can use.

Celebrate the new creation of God!

4.   Write it down for a Memorial

I, _____ (your full name)

gave my life to the Lord Jesus Christ on

_____(month, day, year) at _____(am/pm)

This glorious event took place at _____ (location).

According to *1 John 5:11-12,* I have been removed from Satan's kingdom of darkness and evil and brought into God's Kingdom of Righteousness and Light. I now have eternal life. God Himself, the Righteous Judge of all mankind, has made me righteous in His sight. Therefore, Satan cannot condemn me. Sin no longer has dominion over me. I have power, through the Holy Spirit, to live a life that is pleasing to God.

5. Now what?

Tell someone about your salvation and share this wonderful news every chance you get. As you do, assurance will continue to grow in your heart about what the Lord has done. But, you may ask, why is it important to tell someone that you are saved and that you believe in the Lord Jesus Christ? Here are three simple reasons among many.

First, Jesus does not want you to be a Christian in secret. Right now, you are the only one who knows you are born again. If you are embarrassed or uncomfortable telling another person that you are saved, Jesus interprets that as shame. In *Mark 8:38,* He said, "If anyone is ashamed of me and my words in this adulterous and sinful generation, the Son of Man will be ashamed of him when he comes in his Father's glory with the holy angels." You can see that Jesus considers telling others publicly about your belief in him a vital issue.

Second, when you tell someone else, it reminds you of your commitment to the Lord. Finally, you may inspire others who may not know the Lord to give Him control of their lives and receive forgiveness and eternal life, as you have.

Be baptized in water. Water baptism is a crucial requirement of the process of being saved. Just as Jesus Himself was baptized in water *(Matthew 3)*, we are instructed in *Acts 2:38* and other scriptures to be baptized.

Get a Bible and begin daily Bible study. *Psalm 119:105* says, "Your word is a lamp to my feet and light for my path." God gave us the Bible to provide us with a revelation of His will.

Before we were saved, we did not care about the will of God for our lives. But now that we are saved, it is important to begin to understand how God wants us to lead our lives. As a new believer you can begin to understand God's directions for you by starting with the gospel of John.

As you read the passages of the Bible, pray that the Holy Spirit will help you understand what you are reading and teach you how to apply what you read to your daily life. It is the application of the Word of God that will help you grow in your walk with the Lord.

Start memorizing portions of the Word of God; memorize the references too. As you read your Bible and begin to apply it every day to your life, certain verses will begin to inspire clear spiritual knowledge in your heart. Keep a diary of how God applies these verses in your life. They will help you in at least two ways. They will give you ammunition against attacks of the devil; and they will help you share your testimony with others.

Begin a life of prayer. Involve God in your daily life by talking to Him just as you would talk to any friend.

Find a church home. Pray that the Holy Spirit will lead you to a strong, Bible-believing church where you will learn the ways and the will of God. Visit a few churches and pray the Holy Spirit to give you absolute peace in your heart about the Church in which you are to be planted.

Do not select a church for its beautiful building or its wonderful choir, because the pastor preaches movingly, or because it seems to have a lot of nice young single members, or for any other such reason. Let the Spirit of God direct you. When you find your church, He will tell you.

Find a ministry in your church. When the Lord shows you your new Church home, become involved immediately in some type of ministry within the Church. It doesn't particularly matter which ministry you become involved in; but it is important to make yourself available to the Lord for ministry.

Find a prayer partner, someone in your new church with whom you can pray. The Christian life is not one of individuality, but of community.

If You Need to Renew Your Relationship with the Lord:

If you have known the Lord but have backslid, in your beliefs or your behavior, you need to renew that relationship.

1. Pray this prayer aloud.

> *Dear Lord Jesus, I ask forgiveness for breaking off my commitment to follow You. I pray, Lord, that You will cleanse me of all my unrighteousness. Renew me in the inner man by Your Spirit. Build a wall of fire around me and give me strength to live for You all the days of my life. Amen*

2. Write it down for a Memorial

I, _____ (your full name)

gave my life to the Lord Jesus Christ on

_____(month, day, year) at _____(am/pm)

This glorious event took place at _____ (location).

According to *1 John 5:11, 12,* I have been removed from Satan's kingdom of darkness and evil and brought into God's Kingdom of Righteousness and Light. I now have eternal life. God Himself, the Righteous Judge of all mankind, has made me righteous in His sight. Therefore, Satan cannot condemn me. Sin no longer has dominion over me. I have power, through the Holy Spirit, to live a life that is pleasing to God.

3. Now what?

Tell someone that you are recommitted to the Lord.

Dust off your Bible and start reading it daily.

Start memorizing portions of the Word of God. Start with these: *Romans 3:23, John 3:16, Romans 10:9,10,13* and *1 John 5:11,12.* The verses you memorize will help you in at least two ways. They will provide you with ammunition against attacks of the devil, and they will help you share your testimony with others.

Begin a life of prayer. Involve God in your daily life by talking to Him just as you would to any friend.

Start attending church again and become involved in a ministry within your church.

Find a prayer partner in your new church.

Some of you may already have a personal relationship with the Lord,. However, you may have been through so much disappointment with your desire to be married that you feel like giving up. You need someone to lift up your hands. If that description fits, may I pray for you?

> *Dear Lord Jesus, I bring my brother or sister before you.*
> *I thank you for their salvation and for the fact that their*
> *life is in your hands. Restore to them the joy of their*
> *salvation, open their spiritual eyes, that they can behold*
> *wondrous things from Your Word.*
>
> *Cause their spirits truly to hunger for the wisdom that you*
> *alone can give. May they take hold of Your Word with*
> *new zeal and vigor and may they know in their inner*
> *beings that you will perfect everything that concerns their*
> *lives, and will work everything out for their ultimate good*
> *and for Your glory.*
>
> *Thank you for hearing our prayer. Amen.*

Chapter 1.
Take the Critical First Step

Summary Review Points

1. Develop a personal relationship with the Lord. This is the critical first step for realizing God's will in every area of your life.

2. Understand that marriage is God's will for you.

3. Pursue marriage as a high priority.

Chapter Two

Identify the Roadblocks to Getting Married

"And He did not do many miracles there because of their lack of faith." (Matthew 13:58).

A friend recently told me a parable about a fly trapped in a glass jar. Over and over again, the fly flew to the top of the jar in an attempt to escape, only to collide against the lid. After a lot of pain and discouragement, the fly resigned itself to its fate and lay at the bottom of the jar in defeat. Even after the lid was removed it made no attempt to get out.

In many ways I felt like that fly. For years I had tried every way I knew to find my husband. I fasted, prayed, cried out to God, consulted matchmakers, but to no avail. After years of increasing frustration I began to rationalize my single state. Because I knew that God was good, I began to find high and holy reasons for my continued single status. In other words, I gave up. Like the captive fly, I resigned myself to my predicament, despite the fact that deep inside I longed to be married. If I had continued to hold those beliefs, I doubt that I would be married today.

Perhaps you can also identify with a fly in a jar. You have not lost your desire for marriage, but maybe you have dulled your frustration with assumptions like those I have listed. You look around and see no prospects on the horizon. As the years go by, people around you may be doing one of two things: Some are thoughtless, constantly asking questions and making painful comments: "When are you going to get married?" "How old are you?" "You're not married yet?" (often in incredulous tones). "You're not getting any younger, you know." "You'll get so set in your ways that no one will want you."

Then there are those who feel sorry for you, saying in pious tones, "Just hold on, In God's time you'll get married." "Just put marriage out of your mind. When you're not thinking about it, that's the time you'll run into the guy (or the gal) for you. So just forget about marriage. Keep your mind on the Lord."

Although there is a measure of truth in some of the latter remarks, these people remind me of Job's friends, talking without the full counsel of God. Isn't it amazing how strongly family members and friends (the company we keep) can influence how we think and feel about our single situation? Sometimes we seem to be trying to please other people more than we do God. Often, hoping to find a comfort zone between these two conflicting schools of advice, single people vacillate between frantic searching and passive waiting.

After talking to so many single Christian men and women over the years, I have concluded that there is one reason many don't get married: They hold on to certain assumptions that contradict the Word of God. Instead of trusting God's Word, they find comfort in justifying the reasons why they are still single. Those false assumptions become roadblocks, barriers to their happiness, delaying God's blessing in their lives and causing them unnecessary misery.

Some typical assumptions are:

o **My desire for marriage is a want, not a need.**

o **Maybe God has called me to celibacy.**

o **I can serve the Lord better if I remain single.**

o **I need to make a lot of changes in my life before God will send me a wife (or husband).**

o **No one wants to marry me. I don't measure up.**

o **I haven't met anyone who meets my standards.**

o **Christian men are in short supply.**

o I've waited so long and nothing's happened. Maybe God doesn't want me to be married.

o If I "wait on the Lord," eventually He will send my mate along.

While this is not an exhaustive list of the false assumptions so many singles hold, it is fairly representative. Any assumptions we hold that negate the Word of God cannot be blamed on God. Remember the Lord Jesus said to the Jews that their traditions had made "the Word of God of none effect." *(Mark 7:13, KJV)*. In other words, God's Word is still powerful. God's Word will never return to Him void. He watches over His Word to perform it. But the Bible makes it very clear that we can tie God's hands through our traditions, assumptions, unbiblical beliefs, interpretations, and false applications of Scripture.

Let's go back to the analogy of the captive fly. The fly was genuinely trapped. A solid, tightly clamped lid confined it to the jar. Like the fly, some singles trap themselves with assumptions like those listed above. There comes a time when we must ignore the roadblocks in our paths, and break through the limits they place on our lives.

As we examine these roadblocks in detail, I pray this examination will:

o Help dispel the assumptions that may hinder your marriage plans.

o Refocus your attention on God's promises.

o Inspire you with renewed enthusiasm, energy and determination for your future marriage.

o Draw you closer to receiving the mate God has for you.

Roadblock 1: My Desire for Marriage Is a WANT, Not a Need

Lois, a single woman in her late forties, attends my church. For years she has been actively involved; for a while she was the leader of the single adult ministry. Most people think Lois has found great contentment in being single. Her outward appearance seems to exemplify the scripture that talks about "undistracted devotion to the Lord." At Sunday services she seems almost angelic, caught up in the Spirit and blissfully content in the love she has for her Savior.

Outside church, she is a successful career woman, an administrator for a government agency, well liked and respected by all her colleagues and employees. She lives in a beautiful house, drives a late-model European car, and dresses impeccably.

A year ago, everyone was overjoyed when Lois announced her engagement to a man in our church. Before long, however, she announced that it was off; she and her fiance both realized that they were not meant for each other. Lois has told a few friends that she still wants to be married.

Recently, during a completely unrelated conversation, Lois said, "I believe I'll be married in the next seven years." It seems apparent from this comment and from her conversations with me and other friends that she is desperately lonely and afraid of growing old alone. Still, she does not feel that she should spend a great deal of time thinking or praying about marriage. As she puts it, she does not want to "bother the Lord" with petitions for a mate when there are so many more pressing needs to put before Him. Because God has showered so many blessings on her already, she feels it would be selfish to pray for something she considers a "want" and not a "need."

The Bible makes it clear that God answers prayer. In talking to people like Lois, however, I sense that while many of us believe we can ask God for anything in prayer, others are convinced that there are some things they should not bother God about. People seem to set up categories of things called "wants," and others called "needs." In their minds "needs" have a higher priority with God than "wants," and they categorize marriage as a want. They argue that marriage is not God's highest goal for our lives; it is not an eternal state. After all, Jesus Himself said that marriage does not take place in heaven. "There you have it," they say, "marriage must therefore be a want and not a need." But did Jesus reach that conclusion?

Look up those two words--need and want--in the dictionary. Actually, there is little difference between them; they are used as synonyms for each other. So what's the difference? Perhaps people assume a dimension of urgency, of a "deadline," for needs.

Maybe, even after studying the definitions, you are still not convinced that the two words have little difference in meaning, so let's examine the issue as if there is a difference. Does God supply only our "needs" and not our "wants"? According to the Bible, God supplies both. In fact *Matthew 6:33* shows us that our needs are taken care of and "added to us" as we seek God's kingdom first.

Other verses also point out how God gives us the things that we want. In *Psalm 84:11*, for example, God says, "No good thing will be withheld from those whose walk is blameless." "No good thing" covers both wants and needs. And in *Mark 11:24* we find "...Whatever you ask for in prayer, believe that you have received it, and it will be yours."

Numerous other scriptures show us that God will supply not only our needs, but also our wants. He is Lord of every aspect of our lives, and as Lord, He should be consulted about everything, including what we want. Read *Psalms 23:1, Psalms 37:4, Matthew 7:7-11, John 14:14, John 15:7* and *1 John 5:14 ,15*. Notice that God says He will grant our petitions--the things we want. But He qualifies this statement again and again by saying He will give us anything if we ask "according to His will," and "in His name;" if we "believe" and "abide in Him."

Marriage Is God's Will for YOU.

Marriage is God's will, and you can be sure that it is His will for you, as long as you are not called to celibacy. Indeed, God is the originator of marriage; it is His idea, not man's. It is the Lord God who said, "It is not good for man to be alone. I will make a helper suitable for him" *(Genesis 2:18)*. Nowhere in the Bible has God reversed that declaration. The statement is as valid today as it was when God created Adam and Eve. God further underscores the importance of marriage in *Proverbs 18: 22 (KJV)* which reads: "Whoso findeth a wife findeth a good thing, and obtaineth favor of the Lord."

Paul gives instructions on marriage directly from the Holy Spirit when he says: "I will therefore that the younger women marry, bear children, guide the house, give none occasion to the adversary to speak reproach-fully" *(1 Timothy 5:14, KJV)*. Scripture after scripture makes it clear that God sees a mate as a need and not a want. God did not design marriage as the apple that you can see, but cannot have. It is the apple you can see, have and enjoy.

He does not want people to suffer in loneliness and misery. When Adam was lonely, God didn't say, "Sorry Adam, you have to suffer for a few years." God saw that Adam needed a wife and He provided him with one. God is no respecter of persons and He is ready to meet your needs. God's will is for you to be married. If seeking God's kingdom means seeking His will, then seeking marriage should be one of your priorities.

Perhaps this analogy will help your faith. Someone offers you a glass of cold water, but since you are not thirsty, you do not want to drink it. Suppose, however, you are in the middle of the desert, and have not had water for two days. That same glass of water becomes a strong object of desire; you want it more than anything else in the world. Your life depends on it, and time is of the essence. At this point then, the water has become both a need and a want. So it must be with your desire to be married. You must recognize it as a need and make a determined effort to have it fulfilled.

Roadblock 2. **Maybe God Has Called Me to Celibacy.**

Keith attends our home fellowship group. He has a great zeal for the things of the Lord. As a licensed minister who feels called to be an evangelist, he travels to other churches preaching and conducting workshops and seminars. He combines all of this with a full time job. From time to time in our home fellowship group, singles have requested prayer and the group gets together to pray for them. Once Keith was invited to join the singles in a prayer for marriage, he declined. After one of our home meetings, I asked Keith why he did not want the group to pray for him. He responded that he doesn't have marriage on his mind right now and that he is content just as he is.

Before Keith was saved, he was involved in several long-term relationships with women, none of which worked out. Since being saved, he has been interested in a number of attractive women. He recently had a crush on a young lady from another church in town, but his feelings were not reciprocated. It seems that whenever he finds someone that he is interested in, she is not interested in him. For this reason, Keith has resigned himself to a state of celibacy.

Like Keith, you may rationalize that if you are not married, it's probably because God wants you to be celibate. The Bible supports the idea that celibacy is a gift from God. Jesus had a discussion with His disciples on the subject of marriage and celibacy. He said to them, "Not everyone can accept this word, but only those to whom it has been given. For some are eunuchs because they were born that way; others were made that way by men; and others have renounced marriage because of the kingdom of heaven. The one who can accept this should accept it" *(Matthew 19:10-12).*

"Each man has his own gift from God; one has this gift, another has that" *(1 Corinthians 7:7).* God does not force us into a state of celibacy. Like marriage, it is a gift God gives the children of men without regard to merit. A gift cannot be forced on you. Can you accept the gift of celibacy? If you have a burning desire for marriage, obviously you do not have the gift of celibacy.

Celibacy and singleness are not the same thing. Individuals who are called to a life of celibacy have a unique gift of fulfillment from the Lord. They find true fulfillment in a God-ordained fashion, without marriage as a primary means of human contact. Those who are not called to celibacy, on the other hand, usually desire affection and an intimate relationship in marriage. Singleness, therefore, is not an end in itself for most of us. It is a temporary state of waiting for an expected end, which is marriage.

Some people go to the extreme of calling singleness a gift. Nothing could be further from the truth. The only gift God has expressly said He gives in any male/female relationship is that of celibacy. The timing or fulfillment of the marriage plans of single people cannot be considered a gift from God.

The Idea of "Contentment"

Another issue that is often linked to the question of singleness and the pursuit of marriage is the biblical admonition to "be content." This advice is often supported by scripture taken out of context. Two particular verses come to mind: *1 Corinthians 7:25-28* and *Philippians 4:11.* Let's examine them closely.

23

The Apostle Paul in *1 Corinthians 7:26-28* says, "Now about virgins: I have no command from the Lord, but I give judgment as one who by the Lord's mercy is trustworthy. Because of the present crisis, it may be good for you to remain as you are. Are you married? Do not seek a divorce. Are you unmarried? Do not look for a wife. But if you do marry, you have not sinned; and if a virgin marries, she has not sinned. But those who marry will face many troubles in this life, and I want to spare you this."

Paul was giving specific instructions for a difficult period of time when Christians were being severely persecuted. They were sawn in half, burned at the stake, used as torches, thrown into lion's dens, and forced to endure other atrocities. Even in such a context, Paul made it clear that in his own opinion there was no mandate from God to remain unmarried. In fact, in Ephesians, Paul uses the marriage relationship as an analogy of the relationship between Christ and the church.

In *Philippians 4:11,* the Apostle Paul said, "I have learned to be content whatever the circumstances." This verse is often used to support the argument that singles are to be content, but this application seems to be inaccurate. When Paul was shipwrecked, he must have been miserable and afraid, but he knew it was part of his ministry. When he was imprisoned, when he was stoned, when he was hungry, he knew that he was being called to suffer for the gospel of Christ. What Paul is telling us is that he expects difficulties and trials to come his way as he pursues God's will. But even in the most painful situations, through the inspiration of the Holy Spirit, he is content. Before we blindly quote Paul's words, we must understand what he really meant.

There is no doubt that single people who desire to be married are pursuing the will of God for their lives. When God answers their prayers and fulfills that desire, they are admonished to forsake all others and be bound to their mates. They are to be content with the one the Lord has given them. I believe this is also the basis of God's commandment not to "covet your neighbor's wife" (husband). Coveting the spouse of another seems a clear indication that you are not content with the one God has given you.

Again, *Hebrews 13:5* makes it clear that people with God-inspired needs should be content once those needs are met. When the children of Israel were hungry and thirsty in the wilderness, God did not tell them to be content. He sent them manna from heaven and water from a rock. Only after God had met their needs did He expect them to be content with the food and drink He had given them. But when they looked back to Egypt with longing for the crumbs they had received from the hands of their slave masters, preferring those crumbs to the manna He had sent them, then God grew angry.

Helping Ourselves

If God wants Christians to be content when the legitimate needs that He himself has placed in their lives are not met, then why did He instruct us to pray? Using simple logic, it would be sinful and against God's will to work and pray for change at difficult times in our lives, when He only wants us to be content?

Let's consider some good examples. When you are sick, what do you do? Do you praise God and seek contentment in your illness, or do you seek relief and healing through prayer, doctors, and medicine? Obviously, you do what is needed to be healthy again. Illness is not a condition in which God wants us to be content; the Bible clearly instructs us to pray for healing *(James 5:14,15)*.

Isaiah says that Christ bore our sicknesses and diseases, that He took the stripes on His back for the healing of our ills. If this were not so, then seeking relief from sickness would be a sin. Should a Christian be content when his children are without adequate food or shelter? No one in his right mind would tell people to accept such a situation without a struggle. Sickness, hunger, poverty, all are states in which anyone, including Christians, can find themselves. While God does not put us into misfortune, He instructs us to seek release when we find ourselves in that condition.

For most people, the single state is no different. God wants single people to be married and happy. Yet some people see singleness as a unique condition that must be endured. *Proverbs 18:22* clearly teaches that God grants favor to a man who finds a wife. Who are we to tell Christian singles that they would be better off without this favor of God? No Christian who has seriously thought through the idea of "contentment in singleness" would advocate such a position.

Millions of single Christians in our churches and congregations want desperately to be married. They come to church, sing the songs, participate in the activities, but deep inside they are sad and discontented. When church is over, when families go home together, too many single people go back to their lonely lives.

For too long, the church has pretended that everything is fine for single people. It is true that the church does good work to strengthen marriages and families, but it must also begin to extend real effort toward its single members. Most churches tend to create what I think of as little "leper colonies" for single adults. I call them that because it appears that the idea is primarily to isolate single people and keep them busy, to reinforce singleness rather than prepare people for marriage. Of course it is not the mission of the church to devote all of its resources to the needs of single people. But it must be there for all of those who have a need, and for singles that need is to marry. The church must begin to offer real guidance in helping singles find their mates.

Above all, we must stop making single people who truly want to marry feel ashamed, as if they are acting in an ungodly manner. We must stop implying by our actions that God only meant some of us when He said that man should not be alone. Our notion of "contentment in singleness" does not follow the full revelation of the scriptures. Some of my single friends, after a few painful experiences, either put the idea of marriage on a back burner, or just "don't want to be bothered."

Our friend Andy, in his thirties, met a woman who fit all the criteria he had been praying for in a wife. After a brief engagement, however, she broke off the relationship with Andy and married another man. Then he met another wonderful woman, but she did not reciprocate his interest, and ended up marrying someone else. Twice burned, doubly careful; Andy has deliberately gone into a holding pattern. He has both a full-time and a part-time job, is furthering his education, and is involved in several ministries in his church. Basically, Andy says he is happy, and doesn't think of marriage on a regular basis, at least for now. Andy admits he came to that conclusion not because he doesn't want to get married, but because of his past disappointments.

Andy and thousands like him still desire marriage, but they have been hurt and disappointed so often that they are afraid to try again. When they say they are "content," they really mean it is too painful to stir up false hope. Ben and I have told Andy not to let his past experiences dictate his future actions. As a single person, if you are honest with yourself and really desire to be married, you must throw away the notion of 'contentment in singleness.' Let the promises of God direct you into pursuing all that He has for you and your life. Don't ever settle for less than the best God has for you.

Roadblock 3. The Bible Says I Can Serve God Better If I Remain Single.

Matthew is an evangelist who speaks frequently at our church. He is attractive and charismatic, is a dynamic orator, and has a beautiful singing voice. Single women in the church nearly swoon when he comes. They bring him their best dishes in hopes of getting to talk to him in person. They invite him to their homes. One woman I know even sneaked into his hotel room, declared her love, and tried to persuade him that God intended them to marry. Many women write him letters to that effect, or follow him from one preaching engagement to the next, just to be near him.

Matthew now has people who travel with him whose sole responsibility is to deal with all these admiring women. In spite of all this adulation, he is a man of great moral integrity. Sometimes he jokes about the antics of his most aggressive admirers in his sermons. He does not do it to put them down, but to indicate that he is aware of their motives and not interested. He often remarks that because he is in his mid-thirties and a pastor, many people feel he should be married. But he believes that because of the type of ministry he has, traveling constantly to different churches, and spending so much time on the road, marriage to him would be too much of a strain for any woman. Although Matthew recognizes that he is not called to celibacy, he believes he can serve God better if he remains single at this point in his ministry. He and others find support for that position in *1 Corinthians 7:32-35.*

> *"I would like you to be free from concern. An unmarried man is concerned about the Lord's affairs--how he can please the Lord. But a married man is concerned about the affairs of this world--how he can please his wife--and his interests are divided. An unmarried woman or virgin is*

concerned about the Lord's affairs: Her aim is to be devoted to the Lord in both body and spirit. But a married woman is concerned about the affairs of this world--how she can please her husband. I am saying this for your own good, not to restrict you, but that you may live in a right way in undivided devotion to the Lord."

Looking closely at these verses, we see that they emphasize the potentially greater amount of time a single person has to devote to the Lord's service. Married people, on the other hand, are obligated to spend time with their families. While this is true and biblically based, I don't believe that this portion of scripture is designed to encourage a single life style. Its purpose is to provide a contrast between the states of singleness and marriage. Those who idealize the single state, however, tend to elevate it to a position of superiority over marriage. They seem to imply that married people have somehow forfeited its unique advantages. Those advantages include freedom to go where God leads, to be a missionary or an evangelist, and to devote undistracted attention and service to the Lord.

Perhaps in Matthew's case, this is true. But still, God chose the example of marriage to demonstrate to the world His relationship with His bride-- the church *(Ephesians 5:22-32)*. He also uses marriage and the loving relationship between a husband and wife to teach the world about Himself and His love for us. The simple reality is that single people also become preoccupied with other concerns and activities that can distract them from a life of complete devotion to God.

It is also important to point out the millions of married believers, all over the world, in every area of Christian service and ministry, who serve the Lord with passion and zeal. They include pastors, teachers, missionaries--people performing every imaginable form of service. One notable example is Dr. Billy Graham, a world renowned evangelist who has served the Lord faithfully for more than thirty years. No one would suggest that his effectiveness for God has been diminished in any way because he is happily married.

Throughout history, and to this day, countless missionaries uproot their families and move across the world to serve the Lord, with inspiring results. Is there any justifiable basis for stating that the level of commitment to Christian service of married people is any less than that of single people? From Priscilla and Aquilla, who ministered to Paul's needs, to modern-day families who sacrifice all for the Lord, literally millions of married couples are mightily used by God.

Most individuals are single not because God has called them to be single, but because God is preparing them for marriage. To proclaim that singleness is to be preferred because of its unique "advantages" is to demonstrate tunnel vision. God designed marriage as the norm for the vast human majority.

Roadblock 4. If I Change My Life God Will Send Me a Spouse.

Once I heard a sermon during which the pastor told the single people in his congregation that "the Lord will bless you with your marriage partner when you became a 'whole' person." He explained that those who wish to marry must first learn to be complete within themselves, as single people. His point was that because God puts two whole people together in a relationship, people who are not whole can not come together and produce a healthy, God-glorifying marriage.

Dennis, a friend who had been waiting years to be married, told us he had been really inspired by the sermon. He felt he finally had found the key, declaring, "I'm going to work on myself until I am whole. Then I know God will send me a wife." Because Dennis was so happy, I did not want to question his newfound revelation. But in the back of my mind I was thinking, "How will you know when you are whole?"

No one goes into marriage free of faults or shortcomings. We all have areas that require growth and development. Yet I often hear well-meaning pastors preach fervently that until Christian single people are fully "prepared" they are not ready for marriage. The implication is that singleness is a state of deficiency from which people must be rescued or "redeemed." Those who believe this are indirectly telling single people that they must earn marriage, through good works, prayer, fasting, or other forms of self improvement.

Has no one noticed that married Christian people also have faults? None of us, single or married, is perfect. Personal and spiritual growth can and must take place after we marry as well as before. Thankfully, God does not reward us according to our righteousness, but according to His grace, just as He saved us by grace." For by grace are ye saved through faith; and that not of your selves: it is the gift of God: not of works, lest any man should boast" *(Ephesians 2:8,9, KJV)*.

God also blesses us with grace. He does not treat us as our sins deserve or repay us according to our iniquities *(Psalms 103:10)*. God blesses us wholeheartedly, much as an earthly father blesses his children--despite our faults and shortcomings. "As a father has compassion on his children, so the Lord has compassion on those who fear Him" *(Psalms 103:13)*. Obviously, perfection is not a necessary precondition to finding a husband or wife.

In a good marriage, the strengths of each partner may tend to complement the weaknesses of the other. For example, my husband Ben and I are completely opposite in many ways. I am very detail oriented, Ben has a more global approach to life. While he is looking at the big picture, I read the fine print. I do everything quickly--often without thinking things through, whereas Ben is deliberate and methodical. The funny thing is that even though Ben sees his willingness to take plenty of time as a virtue, it drives me crazy. He agrees with me that my speed and efficiency make it easier to manage our time, and he is learning to speed up a little, just as I occasionally remember to slow down. Our marriage relationship has taught me how "iron sharpens iron."

God uses our differences to help us develop patience, understanding, and tolerance. Ben often jokes that when he was single he felt totally patient and self- controlled. After we got married he discovered that God had given him a better mirror to look into (me) and he realized he was not so patient and controlled after all. A spouse is one of the best instruments God can use to help people grow spiritually and emotionally.

This is not to say that single Christians should not work on personal growth and character development before they marry. But the idea of going into marriage in a state of perfection is not only biblically unfounded but humanly unattainable. No matter what form it takes, personal growth and development is a lifetime process. In seeking a mate, therefore, pray for a person who will:

o See you as the Lord does.

o Love you no matter what your shortcomings are.

o Complement your weaknesses.

o Commit to being a real helpmeet where you are weak.

o Promote and enhance your strengths.

When God gives you a mate who meets these criteria, then you have managed to push this roadblock aside.

Roadblock 5. Who Would Want to Marry Me? I Don't Measure Up

My good friend Michelle has longed to be married for all the years I've known her. When we first met she was dating Glen, who was divorced and had no intention of marrying again. Very much in love, Michelle hoped that time and intimacy would change his mind about marriage. She tried constantly to meet his standards for the perfect woman.

Years went by, and Glen never budged from his position: "Take me and the relationship I offer, or forget about me." Michelle was so dependent on Glen to give meaning and joy to her life, she could not bear the thought of leaving. Then she became a Christian, and was determined to live in a way that was pleasing to the Lord. She knew that her relationship with Glen was an unequal yoking, (*2 Corinthians 4:16),* and that their sexual relationship was a sin.

She encouraged Glen to attend church, and tried to win him to the Lord. Glen, however, thought he was doing just fine. Further, because his first wife had been a member of a religious cult, he was afraid that Michelle had similarly become a "religious fanatic." When he saw the direction Michelle's life was taking, he was more than happy to take off in the other direction.

Michelle became extremely despondent. She missed Glen's companionship, missed having a man to rely on. She met many men at her church, but no one became more than a friend. Michelle began to see the fact that she was deaf as the reason that she was not able to find a husband. Interestingly, Glen and most of the other men Michelle had dated were hearing. Friends tried to convince her that her deafness was no drawback to finding a mate. She was beautiful, intelligent, and personable, and never had any problems meeting and attracting men--hearing or deaf. Men were simply drawn to her. It did seem however, that very few of those men were saved.

A Lifetime Search for Love

Michelle constantly battles loneliness, even as a new Christian with scores of friends. Years of counselling have helped her realize that much of the way she feels about herself is based on the fact that she had been sexually abused as a child. She has strong feelings of rejection and in her own words, low self esteem. All of her life, she says, she's been looking for love. Even the loyalty of her new Christian family, as well as long-time friends, cannot overcome her loneliness. She is fine during the day at work, but coming home to her empty apartment fills her with thoughts of unworthiness and self-pity.

Michelle also battles to win the victory over sexual sin. As a new Christian, she has struggled to give up the intimacy she craves, having felt so rejected as a teenager. For Michelle, sex--even a one-night stand--used to make her feel loved and accepted. When friends try to show her that these relationships are destructive and exploitive, she vaccilates from apathy to depression.

Often, when I talk to Michelle, her first words are,"I'm just so depressed." The bottom line is always "I want a husband." Obviously, despite years of therapy, Michelle still needs to deal with the deeper issues of rejection in her life. She has grown in her relationship with the Lord, but she enters her late thirties still longing for marriage and children. Because so many years have gone by with no prospect in sight, Michelle feels defeated and depressed. She gives new meaning to the word "pity party"--constantly putting herself down.

One week she complains that she is too fat to interest anyone. She goes regularly to the gym to work out. But Michelle is really an attractive woman. The next month, when she gets her weight down to a size that she's comfortable with, she complains that no one wants her because she's deaf. To deal with her depression, she binges on food, puts on weight again, and is even more depressed. This has become an endless downward spiral in Michelle's life, to the extent that last year she occasionally phoned me with threats of ending her life.

Despite all her years of counselling, Michelle still dates men who are not saved. Many men, when they first meet her, profess to be in love with her, but it soon becomes obvious that sex is the major basis of the relationship. Michelle does derive short-term gratification from these relationships. "At least," she says, "I'm not alone. I have someone to hold me in his arms for a night." She feels guilty and depressed each time she falls; she realizes she is settling for second best, and that God must have a better way.

At this point, some readers may wonder whether Michelle is truly saved, since she seems to be continuously trapped in a cycle of sexual sin. For as the Bible says in *1 John 3: 4-6,* "Everyone who sins breaks the law; in fact, sin is lawlessness. But you know that he appeared so that he might take away our sins. And in him is no sin. No one who lives in him keeps on sinning. No one who continues to sin has either seen him or known him."

I do not question her salvation or her commitment to the Lord because I do not know what is in her heart. Nor do I excuse her sin, which she herself readily acknowledges. But I believe lots of people can identify with Michelle's dilemma. She is no different from many other single people with real or imagined deficiencies that become roadblocks, and that hinder them from getting married. In fact, "imagined deficiencies" are very real in the minds of those who hold them, and can be just as detrimental as very real qualities or attributes.

Not Quite Perfect

Some people become convinced that they are too ugly to attract mates; others feel that their physical attractiveness or popularity tend to intimidate members of the opposite sex. Still others are sure they are too short or too tall, too fat or too skinny, too intelligent or too dumb, too poor or too rich. Whatever happens, many people find personal flaws that can explain their single status.

Looking around, it's obvious that millions of people who are "too ugly, too gorgeous, too short, too tall, too fat, too skinny, too intelligent, too dumb, too poor, too rich or whatever--are also married. If they can be married, if someone was attracted to them, believe me--you can be married too. There is someone out there who will love you for yourself, completely and unconditionally, despite your real or imagined flaws.

Morris and Arlene developed a very close friendship at church. Morris is 33 years old and works hard at a good job. Arlene is 43, has a warm, charming personality, and loves the Lord. The two of them are close enough to talk freely about marriage in general terms. Morris is genuinely attracted to Arlene and her good qualities, and would love to marry her. But he feels intimidated by several facts: she is older, earns more money, drives a better car, and lives in a beautiful house, while he rents an apartment. For these reasons, although he is sure she would accept his proposal if he would ask, he is afraid to do so.

Some people might say that Morris lacks courage and is unsure of himself. That characterization may be justified by the fact that he is overlooking the essentials of a good relationship. What he considers important has become a barrier to his happiness. Both Michelle and Morris have trapped themselves into assumptions that are obviously false and that clearly hinder their desire to be together. As children of God, they need to see themselves as God sees them.

Roadblock 6. I Haven't Met Anyone Who Meets My Standards.

This seems to be a common complaint of many singles, women as well as men, especially in this age of professionalism. Many more women nowadays, for example, attend college and hold well-paid professional jobs. They may feel that they should marry men who have similar credentials, or at least move in the same social stratum. For instance, a woman who is a corporate executive wants to know that if she and her husband attend business-related social events she can feel confident that he will get along well with her colleagues. Unspoken societal pressures seem to make it imperative to find a mate who fits a certain profile.

Everybody, it seems, is obsessed with outward appearance, education, and status. We are interested in the kinds of cars people drive, the jobs they hold, their bank accounts, where they live, the schools they attended, their family backgrounds, and other details of their lives. Single people say things like, "I can't date so-and-so, because..."

"...he's just a maintenance worker; I have a degree and a good job."

"...he's too short," or "...she's taller than I am."

"...have you seen the awful neighborhood he lives in?"

"...his car is a clunker. I could never be seen in that. I'd rather take the bus than ride in that car."

"...I want a woman who looks like a model, cooks like Julia Child, keeps the house impeccably clean, and meets all my other needs."

"...can you believe he earned his degree from (blank) university?" (implying that the school is second-rate)

The American media tend to glorify the external, superficial things of life until they become the standard for us all. Slim, beautiful models grace the covers of magazines. Wealth and power seem to be the only identifying marks of success. If we are not being urged to acquire money, dress better, and spend more, we are hearing about people we don't want to be like. Little emphasis is placed on average people, and none at all on the importance of inner qualities.

The daily barrage of overt and subliminal messages about success coerces too many people into accepting these values as their own. Many single people may not even be aware that they are thinking superficially; they just see it as "trying to get the best" for themselves. People who think this way may spend years looking for perfect mates--the answer to their media-based dreams. Anyone who doesn't measure up is swiftly disqualified. Anyone who doesn't make an outstanding first impression probably won't get a second chance. But if everyone keeps looking for perfection, no one will ever get married, because none of us is perfect.

1 Samuel 16:7 says, "The Lord does not look at the things man looks at. Man looks at outward appearance, but the Lord looks at the heart." Shouldn't that also be our attitude toward each other? How many lonely people miss finding a diamond in the rough by relying solely on the evidence of their eyes. It's important to note that the Bible describes Jesus in *Isaiah 53:2b-3a*, in this way:

> *"He had no beauty or majesty to attract us to him, noth-*
> *ing in his outward appearance that we should desire him.*
> *He was despised and rejected by men..."*

Apparently Jesus, who was perfect in every way, could never have impressed us with His appearance. Many of us, if we saw Him in person today, chances are we would reject him. On the other hand, we humans, riddled with flaws and personality defects, are loved and accepted unconditionally by God. In looking for a mate, therefore, pray for someone you can also love unconditionally.

Roadblock 7. **Christian Men Are in Short Supply.**

When people insist that there are not enough single Christian men to go around, they usually have two things in mind. First they imply that very few men are "good" enough for marriage. We dealt with that implication in the last section. Secondly, they hint that statistically, there are many more Christian women than men. Let's deal with that implication here.

My friend Becky was not saved when she first got married. She and her husband had four children--three boys and a girl. After she was saved, her husband basically wanted nothing to do with her "new religion." She did everything, including Christian counseling, to make the marriage work, but ended up divorced with custody of all four children. After all attempts at reconciliation failed, her former husband moved to another state and remarried.

She had a difficult time raising the children by herself, and after a few years, she started asking the Lord to provide another father for her children. Becky was not bashful about her search. While other single women in our church were sitting around complaining about the shortage of Christian men, hoping that husbands would fall from the sky, three different Christian men showed serious interest in Becky, and all three wanted to marry her. One was a physician, the second was a successful businessman, and the third had a good position in the federal govern-ment. Although each man seemed an excellent prospect, Becky turned them all down. She did not believe any of the three was the one for her.

Four years went by. A man we'll call Ed was transfered to Becky's place of work from the Midwest. He was six years her junior, and he worked in a different department, but before long he learned that she was a Christian. They became friends, and within about a year and half, they were married. I was happy to be part of their wedding. Ed adopted

Becky's children, and they now have two more children together. His love for them all is unquestionable, as is the love and respect the children feel for Ed. They are truly one big happy family.

Becky believed and still does that God has no shortages. She had certain criteria for a husband, and she was not willing to compromise. Many of us who knew her were incredulous that she would turn down offers of marriage, especially with four children. But Becky (like Elijah long ago) heard the still small voice of the Lord over the noises of her friends, and she trusted God. Becky knew that God was able and willing to provide for her if she held fast to her confession of faith. Therefore, according to her faith, it was done unto her.

You cannot turn on the television or read the newspaper without being told by self-proclaimed experts that there is a tremendous shortage of men--especially Christian men. As recently as last year, an article on the front page of a national newspaper asserted that a rather substantial percentage of women would never marry in their lifetimes because of the shortage of men. The barrage of negative statistics has slowly sunk into the consciousness of Christian single women. Based on these statistics alone, many have already given up or immobilized their faith.

This assumption that Christian single men are in short supply is addressed to women. Understanding the fallacy of this assumption, however, will also help men develop greater sensitivity to the situation Christian single women face. As Christians, we need to be reminded of God's Word in *Colossians 2:8* (KJV) which says, "Beware, lest any man spoil you through philosophy and vain deceit, after the tradition of men, after the rudiments of the world, and not after Christ." How can we apply this verse to our daily lives as Christians? In order to make that determination, we need to understand specifically what the verse is saying. Let's highlight and expand a few key words in this verse:

Beware: Keep your guard up because some overt or covert danger is lurking in the wings.

Lest: So that you do not....

Man: Fallen, sinful human creatures with all our limitations.

Spoil: To make bad, useless, or barren something that is productive and useful; to destroy something that is otherwise healthy.

37

Philosophy and vain deceit: The false thinking of men.

So *Colossians 2:8:* might be paraphrased: "Keep your guard up; danger lurks in the wings. You must be on guard so that sinful man does not make useless the Word of God that would otherwise be productive for you. For if you let him, man will destroy the seed of God's Word in your life through false thinking and teaching, limited only to what your senses can conceive, never taking into full account the transcendant realities of God's spiritual order."

Taking this verse to its ultimate conclusion, we can understand that the seed of doubt is any information we receive as Christians that causes us to question any Word of God in terms of its applicability, its fulfillment, or the timing of its manifestation in our lives.

You must become spiritually vigilant, my Christian friend. The devil's aim is to ensure that you have less and become less than what God intends you to be. Satan does not have a difficult job stealing God's blessings, delaying the fulfillment of God's purposes, and leading you into sin, once he has succeeded in planting seeds of doubt in your mind and spirit. He did this with Adam and Eve in the garden. He tried to do it with Jesus, but failed. He has not given up on his old trick; it has worked for him from the beginning, almost without fail.

That is precisely why God cautions us in *Romans 12:2::* "Do not conform any longer to the pattern of this world, but be transformed by the renewing of your mind. Then you will be able to test and approve what God's will is--his good, pleasing and perfect will." The Bible goes further to tell Christians how to transform and renew their minds. In *Philippians 4:8 (KJV),* we read: "Finally, brethren, whatsoever things are true, whatsoever things are honest, whatsoever things are pure, whatsoever things are lovely, whatsoever things are of good report; if there be any virtue, and if there be any praise, think on these things."

Using Our Minds

God gave you a mind to help you navigate through this life. He has told you how to get the best use of the mind He has given you. *Philippians 4:8* gives us, as Christians, the tests we need to apply to any piece of information, thought, or fantasy that tries to take root in our minds. If the information meets God's tests, we may embrace it. On the contrary, if it doesn't meet God's tests, He tells us precisely what to do with it. In *2 Corinthians 10:5 (KJV)*, the Bible says: "Casting down imaginations, and every high thing that exalteth itself against the knowledge of God, and bringing into captivity every thought to the obedience of Christ."

God is telling you that your mind is a treasure house containing precious gems, deposits of riches in the form of your knowledge of Christ. Such knowledge is good and helpful to you, so guard it carefully and defend it vehemently. Be alert, vigilant, and watchful, critically examining every "visitor" that shows up at the door of your mind. Your God is so kind and loving that He does not leave us alone to wonder who these visitors might be. He clearly identifies them for us. Chief among the intruders He warns about in this passage are "imaginations and every high thing."

Don't just admit every thought that occurs to you, He is saying, because not all are out to do you good. Some ideas come to strengthen and assist you in the knowledge of Christ. Others come to destroy your knowledge of Christ. God tells us to "refuse admission to those who come to disrupt and challenge the good word of Christ." Admit only those thoughts that reinforce your knowledge of Christ. This is a second-by-second battle, which you must determine to win every time. For those who lose, the consequences are costly.

Very often, Christians seem to have the idea that when Satan tempted Jesus in the wilderness, he literally showed up in his red suit, pitchfork in hand, and engaged Jesus with all the temptations recorded in the gospels. But obviously Jesus, as God in the flesh, had full knowledge and understanding of Satan's pathetic attempts to trip him. Jesus was not "swinging at Satan in the dark." Having studied these scriptures, however, I believe that Satan tried his level best to gain access to Jesus' mind. He worked through thoughts, high things and imaginations. But Jesus refused him admission, each and every time, providing us with an example to follow in our own dealings with Satan.

Therefore, in order to have your desire for a mate fulfilled, you must reject every bit of information, every idea, suggestion, or comment you receive about marriage that conflicts with the Word of God, regardless of who offers it or how logical and pious it sounds. Keep this thought in mind: No one can speak more authoritatively on any subject under the sun than God. "There is no wisdom, no insight, no plan that can succeed against the Lord" *(Proverbs 21:30).*

God Does Not Have Shortages

The notion that there is a shortage of marriageable Christian men is a critical idea that you must reject outright. The Bible tells us clearly that God instituted marriage. It was He who fashioned woman from man's rib and sent her to Adam. It was God who said "It is not good for man to be alone." And that includes you. God is no respecter of persons. If he made a wife to end Adam's state of aloneness, he will find someone for you. He does not want any Adam or any Eve to feel alone. If God provided for Adam, he will provide for you. If you are a woman you are someone's Eve, waiting to be found. God will not base His provision for you on a physical head count, as man tends to do.

Just as in the United States, countries all around the world take a census every ten years to count their populations. Sadly, even with highly advanced computer systems and other technology, those counts are usually miserably inaccurate, with millions of people left uncounted. These inaccurate pieces of information then become the basis for years of so-called expert analysis. Unfortunately, most people seem more eager to give credence to faulty data than to the Word of God. In your wildest imagination, do you suppose that God is seated in heaven wondering how many people live on the face of the earth? According to *Psalm 139:2,* God knows when you sit down and when you rise up. He knows the number of hairs on your head. I confidently believe He even knows how long each strand of your hair is.

Even when human experts cannot tell you where to find your mate, the Lord God Almighty, the Creator of the heavens and the earth and all that is in them, does know. Instead of listening to "experts," give your undivided attention--spirit, heart, and mind--to what God has to say on the subject. You need not give in to the pervasiveness of negative news. Just make up your mind about whose report you are going to believe, whether it is the news media, the "experts," or the Word of God. Let God be true and every man a liar.

It is important to see that the assumption that there is a shortage of men is faulty on two accounts: The first is the implication that God is not able to provide for His people. The second is that the Holy Spirit is not able to bring two Christians together for marriage. As Christians, we believe that each of us came into this world by the purposeful design and the will of God, not by some cosmic accident. The Bible teaches that God knew you from the foundation of the world, and cares enough to die for your sins. God clothes the lilies of the field; He knows the fall of every sparrow. Jesus Himself said that, as Christians, we are more important to God than the sparrows.

Therefore, if God brought you into this world by His design, then before He brought you here, He had a plan for your life. That's why the Bible says God has given us everything that pertains to this life. To say there is a shortage of men is to accuse God of bringing people into the world when He cannot adequately provide for them.

So my question to you, dear Brother and Sister in the Lord, is this: How can anyone believe these things, and also believe in a shortage of Christian men? A shortage is simply the lack or absence of a necessity. Man defines and classifies things in terms of their abundance or scarcity, based on what he can touch, smell, hear, or see.

Let me give you an illustration. We know that the earth's atmosphere is made up of about 20 percent oxygen and 78 percent nitrogen with the remainder, inert gases. That balance is critical to sustain all life on earth. It is further known that the balance is maintained as plants replenish the oxygen that animals use up. Now let's factor in the presence of deserts; few trees grow there, but oxygen is still needed. By the miracle of God's hand, the balance is constantly maintained to sustain life around the world, in the desert as well as the rain forest.

It seems to me that this is a great miracle, yet it is taken for granted. No scientist bothers to measure the levels of oxygen and nitrogen in any specific location; the presence of life is a testimony to the balance. So it is for Christians. The presence of life is evidence of God's power. God has more than enough power to go around. He maintains the balance of people around the world whether you can see them or not. He has enough men to go around whether you can count them or not.

It is nothing more than seeds of doubt from the pit of hell; the same old tired trick of the enemy who keeps asking "hath God said?" God does say what He means and means what He says. *Numbers 23:19* tells us, "God is not a man, that he should lie, nor a son of man, that he should change his mind. Does he speak and then not act? Does he promise and not fulfill?" The Bible says God will provide for all your needs according to his riches in glory. He is Jehovah Jireh, our Provider. For Christians, it is not what we see, but what we believe that brings the blessings of God into our lives. For you to find your mate, you must believe that he or she is really out there, ready to be found. Then make up your mind eagerly to seek the one God has for you.

Another problem with the idea that there is a shortage of men is that it overlooks the role of the Holy Spirit in bringing into fulfillment every single word that proceeds from the mouth of God. Every miracle that Jesus performed while He was on earth happened because the Holy Spirit brought into being the words that proceeded from His mouth. Remember that as Jesus was riding the donkey into Jerusalem, with a jubilant crowd throwing palms at his feet, someone told the people to be quiet. Jesus responded by saying that if the people kept quiet, He would make the stones sing and praise Him. I am certain that Jesus was saying He would instruct the Holy Spirit to breathe life into the stones so that they could praise Him. The Lord is able to do anything at any time.

God Always Provides

When we give the Holy Spirit anywhere near the level of confidence that we put in man's flawed statistics, we free Him to work on our behalf. Throughout the scriptures, God has shown us over and over again what the Holy Spirit can do. God is not trying to prove the Holy Spirit's power to us, but He gives us more than enough examples to help us understand that the Holy Spirit works on this earth, bringing about the fulfillment of His plans. The Holy Spirit always does the impossible. He worked with Elijah to bring life back to a whole army of dry bones. He raised Jesus from the dead. The Holy Spirit's annointing did not leave after Elisha died. As a result, He brought a dead soldier back to life 120 years after his body fell on the dead bones of Elisha *(2 Kings 13)*.

God is not bound by our statistics. When there were no women on earth God created one for Adam; how's that for statistics? You must believe with all your heart, mind, and strength that God is able to provide for you, no matter what you hear. God is capable of bringing your mate, just as He brought Eve to Adam. Whoever is really searching for a life partner can be assured that God will provide.

In *Genesis 24* we read the story of Isaac and Rebekah. God took Rebekah from the city of Nahor in Mesopotamia, to Isaac who was living in the Negev. Rebekah was in the city; Isaac was far away in the desert. In my own case, God brought my husband from another continent--across the ocean--to me in the United States. God is not limited by distance, space, or time. God has no lack of men or women. The cattle on a thousand hills belong to Him. "The earth is the Lord's, and everything in it, the world and all who live in it" *(Psalms 24:1).*

"My God will meet all your needs according to his glorious riches in Christ Jesus" *(Phillipians 4:19).* This verse doesn't say that God will meet our needs according to statistics or the opinions of experts. When the children of Israel were in the desert with no water to drink, some complained about God's "shortage of water." They asked Moses, "Why did you bring us and our children out here to die of thirst?" And God answered by giving them water from a rock!! It seems a conclusive way of proving that He could do anything. And yet when they were thirsty again, they forgot God's miracle and asked the same question.

Remember that Jesus told Martha, "You must first believe then you will see. God **never** responds to "show me first." Those who believe that God is able to supply their needs will receive. According to your faith, let it be done unto you. When all is said and done, it is a sin for any Christian to say that there is a shortage of men. It is like denying that God can spread a table in the wilderness. God created the wilderness, and He can provide whatever the wilderness requires. He is still Lord, and He did not take kindly to questions of His ability to provide when the children of Israel complained to Moses in the wilderness.

Another biblical example comes to mind. Remember how Simon Peter toiled all night to catch fish? After laboring all night without catching even one fish, he and his friends concluded that there was a shortage of fish on that particular day, and at the break of dawn, they gave up.

Then Jesus came on the scene. First he stood in Peter's boat to preach, then He instructed the crew to launch it again and cast their nets at the place He would show them. They caught so many fish that their boat

43

began to sink and they had to call for extra help. Here is my question: Did Jesus know where the fish were all along or did He just command them to be at the spot where He told Peter to cast the net? Did such a large school of fish just "happen by" at that particular time? The answer is obvious: Jesus had everything to do with the fish being there when the net was cast.

Just as He knew where the fish would be when he instructed Peter to cast his net, He knows where your mate is. So instead of listening to nonsense about shortages, focus your attention on receiving the proper instruction and direction from Him as to where, when, and how to cast your net.

For unbelievers it may be true that there is a shortage of men, but it cannot be so for Christians. There is **never** a shortage of anything in God's kingdom. Be convinced of God's ability to supply your needs--not only in your head but more importantly, deep down in your spirit. Then and only then can you be bold in your prayer life and courageous in the face of discouragement. The naysayers will continue to sing the same old songs, no matter how often God provides mates for all who diligently seek Him and believe in Him.

So if for some reason you have received into your spirit the idea that there is a shortage of Christian men, let me tell you, you have been looking in the wrong places. The scriptures instruct us, in *Hebrews 12:2,* "Let us fix our eyes on Jesus, the author and perfecter of our faith..." If you fix your eyes firmly on Jesus, you cannot miss the abundance of His provisions in all areas of your life!

Roadblock 8. God Must Not Want Me to Get Married.

"I've waited so long. Nothing has happened. I might as well give up." Obviously this assumption refers to God's timing for fulfillment of His promises. As a Christian single person, you are convinced that God will send you a mate, yet the years keeping going by. In order not to appear to dictate a time table to God, you may either have given up completely or resigned yourself to perpetual waiting.

My friends Jane and Leslie are Christian single women in their early forties. They have been the best of friends and roommates for years. I met them when I first joined my church fifteen years ago. During this time they have both wanted to get married, but neither has met anyone who seemed to be right.

Each of the women has been in love more than once, and were heart-broken when things did not work out. After years of frustration, they have both learned to cope with their loneliness, basically by never discussing their strong desire to be married, pretending it isn't an issue, and resigning themselves to the fact that they will not be married any time soon. They have settled into a "spinster" lifestyle. They recently bought a house together. I see them in church, and am saddened by the look of resignation on their faces.

If your life is similar to that of Jane and Leslie, don't despair. It is my personal experience that "the darkest hour is just before the dawn." Satan's attacks on our minds come as an avalanche when we're closest to receiving our blessings. Don't conclude that God does not want you to be married just because your prayer is not answered according to your timetable.

There were times in my six years of actively praying for a husband, especially toward the end when I was deeply depressed, I would scream and cry out to God in the middle of the night. At times, I felt I was losing my mind. In fact, one night I dreamed that I was a bruised and battered child hiding from the enemy with only a cap gun for defense. I felt that God--if He had even heard my prayer--must be unwilling to grant my petition. Soon after this dark period, I met my husband. At God's appointed time, you too will meet the person God has for you.

Defeating Disappointment

Another friend, Debbie, was engaged to Randy, a young minister. Everyone in the church was excited about their upcoming marriage. The pastor often commented about them from the pulpit. A few weeks before their wedding day, Randy broke off the engagement. Within a few months he married Beth, another young woman in the same church.

It is obvious now, from the thriving ministry Randy and Beth have built together, that they were meant for each other. But Debbie has still not gotten over the hurt of her broken engagement. She seems to have given up on marriage. She stays involved in numerous ministries in the church to occupy her time and thoughts. But God says, "I know the plans that I have for you" *(Jeremiah 29:11)*, plans to prosper you and not harm you, plans to give you hope and a future."

Even if, like my friend Debbie, you have been deeply disappointed, don't give up on marriage. Go the extra mile in trusting God to send your mate. After you have done everything He directs you to do, then stand and keep standing. You will see the salvation of your God. Your miracle is at hand! Do not throw away your confidence; it will be richly rewarded *(Hebrews 10:35)*. Hold on to the promises of God and continue to do so. Later on, in Chapter 4, we will discuss ways you can speed up the day you will meet the one God has for you.

Roadblock 9. If I "Wait on the Lord," Eventually He Will Send My Mate.

On a recent Sunday after church, our family gathered to celebrate the thirty-ninth birthday of my cousin Louise. Before cutting her cake, Louise thanked the whole family for her surprise birthday party. With tears in her eyes and a trembling voice, she noted that her birthday had actually been the previous Wednesday. Because she had only received a few cards and little attention, she thought everyone had forgotten. She said she had felt so lonely that she questioned whether she was really born on this day. Everyone was deeply touched by her remarks.

Later during the party, I casually asked Louise about her love life. Seeing the look of pain on her face, I quickly regretted my question. She brushed it aside by saying, "Nothing's happening. There's no one special right now, but I know God's timing is the best." Like Louise, many singles are just "waiting on the Lord." Many have been waiting most of their adult lives, yet no husband or wife has yet appeared. Very often, the following scripture reference serves to give them hope:

> *"Delight thyself also in the Lord; and he shall give thee the desires of thine heart. Commit thy way unto the Lord; trust also in him; and he shall bring it to pass...Rest in the Lord, and wait patiently for him (Psalms 37:4,5,7a).*

Some people see these verses as an excuse for idling away the years, doing nothing but waiting for God to answer their requests. They become a passive audience for the "show" to be put on by the Lord. But that interpretation of these verses is not biblically based. *James 2:17* says, "In the same way, faith by itself, if it is not accompanied by action, is dead." God expects action, activity on the part of every Christian, to demonstrate our faith.

Let's try to understand "rest" and "wait" from God's perspective. The first time we find rest used in the Bible, it was God Himself who rested from all His labor. God rested **after** His mission was accomplished. Rest and wait, therefore, do not imply idleness, rather they signify a pause in directed, purposeful activity.

It is interesting to read in the book of *Exodus* how God provided guidance to His people. The thing that always impresses me about *Exodus* is the active involvement of the children of Israel in receiving God's blessings. On numerous occasions, they had to go to war. They had to fight a world of enemies to claim the land that God had promised them, and that pattern is repeated over and over again throughout Scripture.

Reading the book of *Exodus* can remind you of this principle and pattern in God's work. You must be an active participant to receive God's blessings. God made the children of Israel victorious only when they themselves went out to fight their enemies. God did not send them their victory as they lounged in camp. Even in instances that did not require fighting, they still had to be involved in the miracles of God. The fall of the walls of Jericho is a classic case in point. They engaged in the directed activity of God, then they rested from working to knock down the wall, but they achieved the victory that God had promised them. God provided manna in the desert, but the children of Israel had to go pick it up. God provided water from a rock, but they had to go to the fountain and drink. As we move out in faith, believing that the steps of the righteous are ordered by the Lord, God guides us and directs us to the one He has for us to marry.

"For Heaven's Sake, Don't Look Eager"

I think one reason why some singles, especially women, fall into the passive mode is that they do not want to seem preoccupied or obsessed with the idea of getting married. Many authors advance the argument that single people should do everything possible to enhance their single lives, not to put life on hold as they wait for their mate to come along. Driving the point home, some writers convey the impression that many single women become so preoccupied with marriage that they grow antennae on their heads, which tend to scare off potential husbands.

Any time a man crosses their paths, the radar picks him up and determines his approximate location and marital status. Lights flash and sirens wail, "It could be him! It could be him!" They jump into their specially designed man-hunting suits, saddle their horses and go chasing after this new prospect. They hunt him down, throw a rope around his neck, drag him, kicking and screaming, to the altar, put a ring on his finger, and pronounce him married.

Reading some of these books, you get a picture of that single people going through life beating every bush, shaking every tree, peering into in every crack in the wall and under every carpet, hoping to see someone hiding there. They spend every waking moment looking for a mate, and nothing else is of any importance.

A Partnership With God

Obviously this view is exaggerated, but it is true that some people come dangerously close to obsession in the search for a mate. Trying to avoid this aggressive stereotype, others go to the opposite extreme, becoming totally passive. They take comfort in the notion that one day, when they least expect it, they will stumble upon their mates.

Other authors argue that it is irrational for singles to feel incomplete. They emphasize the idea that single people can be fulfilled without marriage, because as Christians, we are whole and complete in the Lord. They seem to argue that this is a valid substitute for the wholeness God designed for men and women to find together.

Numerous verses throughout the Bible make it clear that these two states are not mutually exclusive. God was already an integral part of Adam's life when He observed that it was not good for man to be alone. God visited Adam in the garden; they had face to face communion, with no sin making a barrier between them. And yet God knew the importance of a human relationship. Clearly, the argument about being whole in the Lord, without a mate, is only partially true. It ignores much of what God reveals throughout the Bible.

Now then, the main questions to ponder are: What is the acceptable level of focus that should be devoted to the pursuit of marriage? Is there a reason to approach the quest for a mate in a different manner than the search for a job or other worthy goals in life? Few people would advise you to sit by and hope to stumble upon a job, an education, a house, a new car. You pray, plan, seek counsel and go out looking for these things, believing the Lord will direct your steps.

Of course you do not pursue any of these goals to the exclusion of everything else. Rather, you apportion your time and energies, working to accomplish the basic objective you have set before you as you pursue other worthwhile goals. Looking for a mate should be no different; it does not have to be an all-or-nothing endeavor, and in most cases, it isn't. So if you have been sitting and waiting for God to bring your husband or wife, start praying. Give "feet" to your prayers in specific ways that will bring glory to God.

Having read the personal histories cited in these pages, I am sure you recognize some of the roadblocks you have stumbled over, and can probably think of others. The bottom line is, will you let anything stand in the way of your getting married? Are you willing to hold on to assumptions that will prevent you from claiming all that God has in store for your life? Face it, as long as you rationalize and make excuses for the fact that you are not married, you will remain in your single state.

Remember, doing nothing at all about the situation brings you no closer to a solution. Rather it entrenches you where you are, making it even more difficult to move ahead. But if you can agree to work with God and get rid of these fallacious assumptions, you will be taking your first great strides around, over, and through the roadblocks in your path.

Chapter Two.
Identify the Roadblocks to Getting Married.

Summary Review Points

1. Identify the rationalizations many singles adopt to explain their single status.

2. Recognize that these rationalizations or false assumptions are not biblical and can become hindrances to getting married.

3. Avoid these roadblocks and go on to receive your marriage partner.

Application Worksheet

1. Do any of the assumptions in this chapter apply to you? Explain.

_____

_____

_____

_____

_____

2. Have your assumptions changed after reading this chapter? How?

_____

_____

_____

_____

_____

3. What do you plan to do about these assumptions?

_____

_____

_____

_____

_____

4. Have you settled in your own mind that God truly wants you to be married? Explain.

_____

_____

_____

_____

Chapter Three

Pray Effectively

"If you believe, you will receive whatever you ask in prayer" **(Matthew 21:22).**

In the last chapter we explored the scriptural foundations that can help single people deal with some of the false assumptions that become roadblocks to getting married. Now that we have identified these barriers, we need to move beyond them.

Now is the time to begin praying. You can accomplish more through prayer than any other way. God knew from the foundation of the world that you would encounter the situation in which you find yourself. He knew you would want to be married; He gave you that desire. He also knew who you would marry. As Christians, we can call on God to use His resources on our behalf, to take care of our problems and our needs. Prayer should therefore be our first priority in every course of action.

Mark's Story

I know my friend Mark wishes he had spent more time praying for God's guidance. Mark's family and mine lived next door to each other as we were growing up, and he and my brother Gregory were best friends. Mark's parents had a problem marriage, and both drank rather heavily. Whenever Mark's father was away on business, his mother was unfaithful; the whole neighborhood knew about it.

While Mark was in college, he became a Christian. He attended a small church and became active in several ministries. One day the pastor told him that the Lord had revealed to him that Mark was supposed to marry

53

Judy, a young woman in the congregation. Mark recalls that even as a new Christian, he was uncomfortable with the idea that God had revealed to the pastor the person he was to marry without also telling him.

Feeling, however, that they should "obey" the pastor's wishes, he and Judy were married. For the first year of their marriage, everything seemed fine, but that changed dramatically after the birth of their first daughter. They argued constantly, never seeming to agree about anything. Because of his difficult upbringing and the problems he had seen in his parents' lives, Mark was determined to make his marriage work.

By the time their third child was born, however, he and Judy had so much conflict in every aspect of their life together that she filed for divorce. Mark did not want the divorce, but he had little choice. Shortly thereafter, they each moved to different states; Judy took the children. That was nine years ago. To this day, Mark has not come to terms with his marriage, his divorce, and the loss of his children.

Seeking Guidance

Too often, people make major life decisions--looking for a job, an apartment, a new car or a mate--by attempting to reach a solution on their own, without consulting the Lord. Yet *Proverbs 3:5 (KJV)* says "Trust in the Lord with all thine heart; and lean not unto thine own understanding. In all thy ways acknowledge him, and he will shall direct thy paths."

For Mark, the lack of prayer and personal guidance from the Lord before his marriage proved disastrous for everyone involved. I am sure most of us remember times in our own lives when we wish we had prayed a little more. Ben and I have purchased two cars--one new and one used. Both turned out to be "clunkers," probably because we did not seek God's direction. We paid dearly in the end for those mistakes. We have since learned to lay out every decision before the Lord and wait for His peace, His wisdom, and His instruction *(Psalms 32:8)*.

We need to pray because prayer is the most powerful instrument for change in any situation. "The prayer of a righteous man is powerful and effective" *(James 5:16b)*. In fact, Ben and I have now developed the habit of praying even about what might seem to be the most trivial matters. We pray when we lose our keys and when we need a parking space in our busy metropolitan area. We have learned that getting into the habit of praying for small things, and seeing God answer, makes it less difficult to expect God to do the bigger things.

> "Then you will call upon Me and come and pray to Me
> and I will listen to you. You will seek Me and find Me
> when you seek me with all your heart. I will be found by
> you, declares the Lord." *(Jeremiah 29:12-14a)*

Although God encourages Christians to pray and promises to answer, few of us pray as much as we ought, or we become weary and give up too soon. The staggering divorce rate--even among Christians, one out of every two marriages now ends in divorce--attests to the fact that not much prayer is going into the important decisions involved in finding and keeping our life partners. How can we be sure that "someone" is the right one? Many men and women "fall in love" with outer beauty, with affluence, status, talent, and other qualities.

"Fall in lust" might be a more apt description. We are deluded by our own desires. When the initial attraction no longer commands attention, the marriage dissolves. When the money goes, health fails, the job is lost--so goes the marriage. Marriage must be based on commitment, first to God and then to each other, not on superficialities.

Prayer provides evidence of our trust in God and His ability to meet our needs. Prayer helps us ensure the result God intends--in this case, finding the mate He intends for us. "We can have this confidence in approaching God: If what we request is according to His will, he hears us. And if we know that He hears us, we also know that we will receive what we ask of him" *(1 John 5:14-15)*.

Harbor No Offenses

You must not go to the Lord with any unconfessed sin in your life. First confess all your sins, and mend your broken relationships. "If I had cherished sin in my heart, the Lord would not have listened, but God has surely listened and heard my voice in prayer. Praise be to God, who has not rejected my prayer or withheld his love from me!" *(Psalm 66:18-20)*. David clearly understood the impact of sin on his relationship with the Lord. Sin cuts off our line of communication with God.

God has given us a pattern to follow as we pray. In every verse where God asks us to bring our problems to Him, He specifically instructs us in the proper way to present those petitions. First, we must seek forgiveness from those with whom we have broken relationships. We must not harbor anger or bitterness toward anyone. God says that if we do not forgive those who offend us, and seek reconciliation, He will not listen to our prayers. God is very serious about this. He says that if you have an offering on the altar and remember that you have an offense against someone or someone against you, you must settle the matter before you can present your offering.

A word of caution, however, to those who may need to resolve troubled relationships with unsaved ex-boyfriends or girlfriends. The idea is not to restore ungodly relationships, rather to eliminate any enmity or offense between you. Be careful that your attempts to make peace do not place you in a vulnerable situation.

My friend Missy, for example, dated a fellow we will call Joe, for several years in college. That was before she was saved, but when she became a Christian, she broke off the relationship. Joe married someone else, but after two or three years, Joe's marriage fell apart. During the process of getting divorced, he and Missy ran into each other and exchanged phone numbers. Before long, he started calling her regularly.

At first, Missy was pleased at the chance to put behind them the hurt feelings left over from their relationship. She told friends that she had no intention of dating Joe again, since he was not saved. Within a few months, Joe professed that he was now saved and Missy agreed to marry him. Eventually it became apparent to everyone that Joe wasn't really saved. He had only claimed to be saved so that he could be with Missy.

Come to Him with Thanksgiving and Praise.

Giving thanks to God focuses our attention on His goodness. Thanking and praising Him helps us remember how great He is, that He is sovereign, and that with Him, nothing is impossible. Recounting the things God has done for us in the past helps restore our confidence that He will come through for us again. Giving thanks and praising God are ways to encourage an attitude of heart that can help strengthen our faith and lift our expectations.

Our prayers must conform to the Word of God and to biblical principles. God instructs all Christians to study the Word. It is not difficult to pray in conformity with the Word of God and biblical principles, if you know the Word. Take time to study what the Word teaches us about marriage and families. What principles, guidelines, patterns and examples do we need to follow? Armed with that knowledge, you can then pray with confidence, knowing that you are praying back to God what He has already revealed. You can also pray with assurance that He will answer.

Pray for God's Wisdom

Like many singles, Walt seemed to have no game plan for finding a wife, except maybe the "hit and miss" method; he hits on a Miss and he misses. Walt met Deanna at a New Members class in his church. They became friends, and eventually Walt became seriously interested. Deanna, on the other hand, was contented to remain "just friends." Walt was heartbroken when Deanna married someone else and moved away.

Soon after, Walt met another woman in the church, and because he so desperately wanted to be married, he quickly proposed. Not surprisingly, his abrupt proposal scared her off. Then Walt developed a long distance pen-pal relationship with a third woman. In a short while, he proposed by mail. The woman accepted. Walt flew out to meet his new fiancee, and was terribly disappointed. The wedding plans were cancelled. What is Walt doing wrong?

Walt's story illustrates the importance of the biblical admonition to trust in the Lord and lean not on your own understanding. Can he succeed if he continues on this course? The Word clearly says that he needs to seek the wisdom of God.

What is wisdom? Wisdom is having full knowledge and understanding of the causes and effects in any given situation, accompanied by the ability to take the right course of action to achieve the desired result. When wisdom is manifested in any situation, the end result is that the person receives all the blessings of the situation, without the disadvantages.

The statement, "pray for God's wisdom" is far more than a cliche. It is crucial to accomplishing your objective--finding and marrying the person God has for you. Remember that wisdom is the right arm of God, or as

Proverbs 3:19 puts it: "By wisdom the Lord laid the earth's foundations, by understanding he set the heavens in place."

When you set out on any important endeavor--seeking a spouse, for example--you need the wisdom of God on your side. Most people don't know the proper way to pray for a husband or wife. Throughout the book of Proverbs, God emphasizes the need to seek and pursue wisdom. Solomon understood that in order to fulfill God's plan for him, he needed wisdom, and God rewarded him greatly when he prayed for wisdom. That is why it says in *James 1:5*, "If any of you lacks wisdom, he should ask God, who gives generously to all without finding fault, and it will be given to him."

It is important to remember that God also provides the qualities of the wisdom He promises to believers. God says that His wisdom is "first of all pure; then peace-loving, considerate, submissive, full of mercy and good fruit, impartial and sincere" *(James 3:17)*. So before you start seriously looking for a husband or wife, pray for God's wisdom and God's solution.

Pray for Knowledge and Understanding

How interesting that wherever the Bible encourages us to seek wisdom, it almost always adds the admonition to seek knowledge and understanding as well. Pondering the relationship among wisdom, knowledge and understanding, I have come to understand that they are inseparable. As Dr. Robert A. Cook, former Chancellor of the Kings' College used to say, "it is important to put a handle on the Word of God." What are knowledge and understanding? Knowledge is having all the relevant information we need in a given situation; understanding is knowing the full implications, the scope and impact, of that information.

Now then, you must pray for God's knowledge and understanding in every situation. Ask God to reveal the falsity of the assumptions that delay your blessings. For instance, the Bible says that God has not changed and still heals people today. But for those who do not believe, He will not be a Healer. As a step of faith, ask the Lord to give you understanding and divine spiritual knowledge of how you must pray for your future spouse. Call to God and He will answer and tell you great and unsearchable things you do not know.

Pray for Discernment and Spiritual Alertness

Let's first agree on brief definitions of these two terms. *Discernment* is the spiritual quality of being able to distinguish between true and false, between that which is whole and that which lacks wholeness. It also includes the ability to use that knowledge in a positive manner. *Spiritual alertness* is the ability to evaluate the spiritual implications and the consequences of any situation, and to factor in those implications and consequences as you respond to that situation.

The story of Joseph shows us how to tie wisdom, knowledge, understanding, spiritual discernment and alertness together. *Genesis 41* talks about Pharaoh and his dreams. Those dreams provided Pharaoh with partial knowledge, but his knowledge was not complete because he did not understand the message or how to make it work for him.

God used the situation to free Joseph from prison. He gave Joseph the wisdom, knowledge, understanding, and discernment to interpret Pharaoh's dreams. Joseph's explanations provided Pharaoh with an additional measure of wisdom, and Pharaoh realized that working with God would let him take advantage of the situation. He was also discerning enough to put Joseph in charge of the coming crisis.

In the end, everything came to pass as Joseph had said. Because he had called upon Joseph to solve the problem, Pharaoh became wealthier and more powerful. He had received wisdom, knowledge, understanding, and discernment, and he had acted wisely. Rather than being destroyed by seven years of famine, he became famous and respected throughout the world as people from all nations came to Egypt to buy grain.

What would have happened if Pharaoh had responded differently? Let's imagine that as Joseph was interpreting the dreams, a respected court magician came along and said, "Long live Pharaoh! Do not believe this man; he is nothing but a jailbird. No such disaster shall happen in your kingdom. You are Pharaoh! The banks of the Nile are rich and fertile. We can always produce more food than the people can eat. Send this Hebrew boy back to prison and let's throw a big party fit for a king!"

Suppose Pharaoh, in a moment of foolishness and pride, had listened to that advice and done nothing. God's word would still have come to pass. The famine would have ravaged the land and its people. Millions would have died in Egypt and in other nations. Pharaoh would have received some knowledge, but little understanding, discernment, or wisdom. Instead of receiving blessings, he and his people would have suffered the full impact of the famine. As Christians, we must pursue wisdom, knowledge and understanding, discernment and alertness all at the same time.

Knowing True from False

As you draw closer to the day you will meet your husband or wife, be certain that Satan will try to distract you by sending counterfeits and fakes your way. You will need the wisdom of the Lord to find the mate God has for you. It's vital to be able to distinguish between someone to marry and the one spouse God intends for you. Satan will try to create situations that will distract you from God's purpose. You need to pray, therefore, for a spirit of discernment. The enemy of your soul may come as an angel of light. You must be able to sense his presence and activities, and therefore to resist him.

> "Do not believe every spirit, but test the spirits to see whether they are from God" *(1 John 4:1)*.

> "Be self-controlled and alert. Your enemy the devil prowls around like a roaring lion looking for someone to devour" *(1 Peter 5:8)*.

The tricks of the enemy have not changed, but we are sometimes blinded by circumstances and unaware of what is going on around us. Spiritual alertness will help us stay vigilant. Factor in the spiritual consequences of your marriage decision. How will you know that Satan is trying to throw you off? First we must know that God would not do anything that violates His Word. For example, if you pray for a husband or wife and you are a Christian, God will not send you an unbelieving mate. He makes it very clear, in *2 Corinthians 6:14,* that Christians should not be unequally yoked with unbelievers.

The Bible also states that unbelievers are in the kingdom of darkness. Whether they are aware of it or not, they are totally under the influence of Satan's evil. As a result, instead of receiving God's blessings, they receive His curses. There are other major spiritual differences between unsaved individuals and born-again believers. God knows fully the effect of those differences, and He instructs His children not to become involved in such relationships. Be sure of this point: God will not answer your prayers by sending you a mate who is not saved. He does not trick us into committing sins against Him.

Nor will God lead you to a married person in your search. His word clearly teaches against adultery. Becoming involved in a relationship with someone who is already married violates God's laws. You may hasten the destruction of a marriage, or end up in an adulterous relationship, both of which God opposes. As Jesus said, "what God has put together let no man put asunder."

You may wonder, at what point is a person not married? My personal opinion is that someone who is widowed or has never been married is not married. Anyone who has been married, and does not have a completed divorce decree is still married. Separation, formal or informal, is just that: separation. People who are separated from their spouses are still married, and even divorced couples often reconcile. Be careful to seek God's full counsel before venturing into such a relationship.

Not long ago, I heard the story of a single woman who asked a well-known evangelist to pray for her. Before he agreed, he wanted to know what her prayer requests were. She told him that the Lord had revealed to her in a dream that she was to marry a certain man. Unfortunately, the man was already married and she wanted God to help her decide what to do. The evangelist refused to pray with her for that petition. Instead, he took the time to walk her through the Bible and explain why God would never answer such a prayer.

Be sure that you are not deluded by lust. *James 4:3* says, "When you ask, you do not receive, because you ask with wrong motives, that you may spend what you get on your pleasures." Let the Holy Spirit of God guide you in your decisions. For the day will certainly come when we must all stand before God and give an account of all that we have done. Will the Lord be pleased? Would you receive a reward for that decision if that were all He was judging you on?

Praying in the Spirit

There may be times, even in the midst of prayer, when you remain somewhat confused. You desire more than anything for your prayer to be from the heart of God, but you are not sure whether your prayer conforms to God's will for you. That is the time to pray in the Spirit.

> "...The Spirit also helps in our weakness. We do not know what we ought to pray for, but the Spirit himself intercedes for us with groans that words cannot express. And he who searches our hearts knows the mind of the Spirit, because the Spirit intercedes for the saints in accordance with God's will" *(Romans 8:26-27)*.

Ask the Spirit of God to help you pray the prayer that will cause your breakthrough. As Christians, it is critical to be able to differentiate spiritually among the things we are praying for just because we want them and the things we are praying for because God has given us peace about them. When we make that distinction, then as scripture instructs us, we can come boldly to the throne room of God for help in time of need.

The effectiveness of Jesus' ministry here on earth is underscored by this statement: "I can of mine own self do nothing; as I hear, I judge; and my judgement is just; because I seek not mine own will, but the will of the Father which hath sent me" *(John 5:30, KJV)*. So instead of wasting years of your life praying for things that God does not want for you, do the smart thing. Go to the Lord first and let Him refine your requests. Then you can safely present those requests back to Him.

Praying Specifically

Now that you have asked for divine wisdom, knowledge and understanding, and have allowed the Spirit of God to speak to you, it is time to begin praying specifically for your marriage partner. This is important because everything God does is perfect to the last detail. He doesn't do things haphazardly. In *Exodus 35-40,* for example, God gives detailed descriptions for building the Tabernacle of Moses. He specifies materials, content, length, breadth, height, shapes, colors, weights, priestly garments, and other important details. When we consider the building of Noah's ark, the temple, creation itself, or anything the Lord does, we can appreciate His abiding interest in details.

On many occasions, when he was asked to heal people who were sick, Jesus asked them, "What do you want me to do for you?" *(Matthew 20: 32)*. Why would Jesus ask such a question when He could see they were ill and needed healing? The answer is simple. Jesus wanted them to state what they wanted in concrete terms. Many Christian singles ask God to send them a spouse, but without giving Him enough details to act upon. If, for instance, you prayed vaguely for a husband, and two fine Christian men showed up at your door showing interest in you, how would you know which was the right one? Would you toss a coin? Or would you judge by their outward appearance?

When Abraham sent a servant to seek a wife for his son Isaac *(Genesis 24)*, he set specific criteria. The woman could not be a Canaanite, but must be from Abraham's country and his own people *(verse 3,4)*. Abraham told the servant that an angel would lead him directly to the woman *(verse 7)*. She would be found on a given day *(verse 12)* and would say certain things *(verse 14)*.

God wants your prayers to be specific, so that you will recognize the answer when it comes. Write down your prayer requests, listing the characteristics you want in a mate. As you pray over the list each day, God will show you how to modify whatever does not conform to His will for you. God says He will give you the desires of your heart, so don't be afraid to tell Him exactly what you want. *James 4:2b* says "you do not have, because you do not ask God."

Making a List

Our friend Tony, a missionary pilot, is praying for a woman who meets the following description: she will have a gap between her front teeth (a trait he finds attractive). She must be a medical student and willing to go into the mission field. She must be older than he is, left handed, and speak at least two languages. Tony is firm about looking for these characteristics, but he also asks the Lord to help him modify the list to reflect His own will.

Tony has met several women who met almost all of those criteria. One woman was in her final year of medical school and four years older than he was. He thought she might be his wife, even though she did not meet the language requirement. At first he rationalized the possibility that she might meet all of his criteria at some future time, but God showed him she was not the one. Tony's list is not cast in stone; he is willing to modify it as God directs.

One of my friends says, "God knows what is best for me. I'm not picky or choosy. Whoever God sends is fine." She may have a point. God does know what is best for us, yet He still wants us to ask. When you give Him something to work with, you also set up a frame of reference to judge whether the person who comes your way is from God or not.

In my own case, I prayed for a man with very specific characteristics. My husband, on the other hand, prayed only for God to give him total peace, unconditional acceptance, and love for the person he was to marry. He had prayed this for so long that it led him to reject other choices along the way. He says that he knew, almost as soon as we met, that I was the one for him. To this day, Ben insists that his commitment to me was spiritual before it was emotional. He knew me first in his spirit, not in his mind or emotions.

My Own List

Before I began to pray in earnest for my future husband, I listed the most important qualities and characteristics I wanted him to have:

o   He must be born again and Spirit filled, mature in the Lord, balanced in the faith, and must love to study the Word.

o   He must be good father material: a hard worker, mature and responsible.

o   He must be a college-educated professional with a master's degree, and more intelligent than I am.

o   He must have a friendly, affectionate, down-to-earth personality.

o   He must love to travel, and must speak French.

o   He must be my age or older, up to age 36 (I was then in my late twenties).

o   He must be five feet nine or ten inches tall, well groomed and attractive, with a good physique.

As I prayed, I found that some of the things on my prayer list became less important. I began to eliminate and modify a few of the items,

64

circling the details I was less committed to finding. For example, one day I noted in my prayer diary that I felt uncomfortable about the criterion for height. I did want to be able to look up to him, but given my height of four feet, eleven inches, he didn't have to be five feet nine or ten inches tall. So for some reason--I now know it was the Holy Spirit's prompting--I changed it to five feet six inches. And that's exactly how tall my husband is--five feet, six inches! Except for the master's degree, all of the other specifications on my list, including those I had marked as not essential, added up to a perfect description of my husband.

The Bible states that Abraham believed God and it was counted unto him for righteousness. Throughout his life, Abraham demonstrated the precious quality of seeing things from God's perspective. The promises of God became more than meat and drink for him. Even as he tried to "help God" fulfill His promises, he never wavered in his faith that those promises would come to pass. He held onto them; he called them into being; kept them in the forefront of his mind and continually reminded God of His promises. Through this attitude, Abraham "called those things which were not as though they were."

In the same way, I began to see my future husband every day with the eyes of faith. After I was satisfied that my list represented accurately what the Lord had put in my spirit, I began to thank God for this unknown man. I felt as though he existed in my life, and I held on to him in spirit. I prayed that God would bless him on his job, bless him financially, help him continue to grow spiritually, and send him to me soon.

I also prayed for the attitudes and skills that would make me a good wife. I asked God to help me learn to cook, to manage my money more efficiently, and to adopt a submissive attitude. As I focused on those prayers, I felt increasingly expectant and joyful. My situation no longer seemed hopeless. I began to see possibilities, to know that God is bigger than my needs. I prayed with assurance.

Your Life, Your Prayers

At this point, a word of caution: please do not use my criteria as a yardstick to measure everyone who comes your way. Let the peace of God reign in your heart and help you set your own standards for your future mate. God will do whatever He promises you. Secondly, do not fail, after asking God to help you set criteria for a mate, to pray

65

earnestly and present them to the Lord. Praying your criteria back to the Lord is the surest way to receive your mate.

Never give in to the feeling that time is passing you by. If you want a lifetime partner and God's best for you, resolve to work with Him. Don't become desperate enough to marry the first person who comes along. Wait for the one who fits the description that you and the Holy Spirit have agreed upon. You have gone through the process of laying your request before the altar and allowing the Holy Spirit to refine it, so stand firm. Then pray, pray, pray, and be confident that God will give you the desires of your heart.

Bombard Heaven with Your Fervent Prayers

Marriage is important. You cannot pray casually for something as crucial as your future mate. Put your whole heart, mind, soul, and body into your prayers. Walk boldly into the throne room of God every time you pray for your mate. Be determined to get God's attention.

Remember the story of the two blind men? *(Matthew 20:29-34)*. Intent on having their sight restored, they refused to listen to the crowd that admonished them to be still as Jesus passed by. Had they not called to Him over the noise of the crowd, they would have remained blind despite the fact that they had come so close to Jesus the Healer. But they would let nothing come between them and God's mercy. Sometimes we must shout, be agressive, push the naysayers aside, do whatever is necessary to grab God's attention.

Jesus gives us a perfect example of what it means to get God's attention. *Hebrews 5:7* records that "During the days of Jesus' life on earth, he offered up prayers and petitions with loud cries and tears to the one who could save him from death, and he was heard because of his reverent submission." Jesus prayed with intensity, "with loud cries and tears." He prayed with purpose and determination. He prayed knowing that His life depended on it. He spent the time necessary to hear from God and always valued the will of God above His own. Bombard heaven with your prayers. Let God know you mean business!

Pray without ceasing *(1 Thessalonians 5:17, KJV)*.

In *I Samuel 1,* Hannah prayed for a child earnestly and without ceasing.

She was not shy about expressing her need; she prayed with crying and weeping and intensity of heart, and did not give up until she received an answer. Her persistence was effective. God heard and responded; He gave her a son.

I persisted in my prayers for six long years. Looking back now, I think the time might have been shorter if I had learned earlier some of the spiritual lessons in this book. In *Luke 11:5-8* and *Luke 18:1-8,* Jesus applauds the persistence of those who petition the Lord, and attributes God's answers to the fervency and sincerity of their prayers.

Finding and marrying the person God has for you depends largely on your prayers. Pray "in season and out of season." Pray when you are happy and even more fervently when you are sad and down. Pray for your mate whenever you feel alone. Pray until you receive peace in your heart and spirit, assurance that your voice has reached the throne of God and your petition has been answered.

Read *Philippians 4:8* for the litmus test of prayer. If ever you are confused about how well you are praying, check your prayer against that verse. Pray until you get God's attention and He says, "Get up from your praying and do something about your situation!"

This is a a good time to make a list of specific qualities you will expect and things that will confirm the answer to your prayer for a husband or wife. You may be surprised at how comforting it is to have a specific description of the one you seek.

The Qualities and Characteristics I Want in My Future Spouse Are:

_____

_____

_____

_____

_____

_____

_____

Chapter Three: Pray Effectively

Summary Review Points

1. Realize that prayer provides the evidence of your trust in God and His ability to meet your needs.

2. Use prayer as the most powerful tool for getting an answer to your request.

3. Pray for God's wisdom, knowledge and understanding, for a spirit of discernment and for spiritual alertness.

4. Be sure your prayers conform to the Word of God and do not violate His principles.

5. Pray in the Spirit.

6. Pray specifically: Write down your criteria for a mate.

7. Pray for the Holy Spirit to help you refine your criteria.

8. Bombard heaven with your fervent prayers.

9. Persist in prayer until you know you have broken through to God and it is time to do something.

Author's Note: See the back of this book for information about how to order a copy of the *Believe God For Marriage* **Prayer Journal.**

Chapter Four

Act on Your Prayers

"But be ye doers of the word, and not hearers only, deceiving your own selves" (James 1:22, KJV)

There are basically three kinds of people in this world: there are problem-oriented people, there are solution-oriented people, and then there are those who sit on the fence and are blown about by every wind that comes by. Which kind of person are you?

For a long time, I was problem-oriented. For six years, I prayed and waited for something to happen. Years went by, and it seemed my prayers would never be answered. I envied my friends who were married and had families. Sometimes I drifted into self-pity, even depression. Occasionally I became very mystical about my hopes for marriage, expecting God to drop my husband from the sky. *Psalm 37:7,* says "Rest in the Lord, and wait patiently for him." Like a lot of single people, I believed that meant I should sit home and wait for my husband to find me. I was "waiting on God."

One day my pastor told me the story of how he met his wife. When he decided it was time for him to marry, he made up his mind that he would not marry anyone from his own church. Whenever he had an opportunity, he would visit different churches and ask the pastor to introduce him to the "best women" in the congregation. He dated several young ladies from many different churches, but he did not meet anyone who met his criteria for a wife.

Meanwhile, a young woman named Cindy, who was his sister's best friend and a member of his church, seemed always present in his life.

She spent so much time around his house that she seemed part of the family, and in fact, he came to think of her as a slightly pesky younger sister. People in the church tried to get them together, but he was not interested. Cindy, however, was very much interested in him, and she found appropriate ways to let him know. Eventually, after scouring other churches for a wife to no avail, he began to see Cindy with new eyes, and recognized that she was indeed the woman he was to marry.

Listening to his story, I realized I had never really given "feet" to my prayers as he and Cindy had. Although he did not find a wife through his search in other churches, the fact that he actively pursued his wish to be married helped him recognize the mate who was literally right under his nose. And Cindy, without being overly aggressive, chose to be honest about her feelings rather than wait and hope he would notice her.

My pastor's experience helped strengthen my understanding that resting, from God's perspective, involves "directed activity." I learned that, with God's direction, I could actively pursue an answer to my prayers. Resting does not mean sitting idly by. Rather, it means doing what God directs that will help bring an answer to your prayers. You must work to get a husband or wife just as you would if you were pursuing a job or a college degree or any other goal.

Taking Action

The Bible makes it clear that the faith of Christians must be accompanied by specific action. Throughout Scripture, we see God-inspired action, taken by people who vigorously demonstrate their faith in God's power to answer prayer. Of course God can answer prayers without our participation, but He calls us to get involved in solving our own problems. Clearly, God wants to use our own desires to help develop our faith. When we pursue actions as God directs, we find greater joy in receiving the ultimate blessing.

Let's examine a few biblical role models--individuals who took action to find answers to their prayers.

o   A widow diseased with an issue of blood for 12 years touched the hem of Jesus' garment and was healed *(Matthew 9:20-22)*..

o   Moses stretched out his hand over the Red Sea, and God divided the waters to set the Israelites free *(Exodus 14:16-22)*..

o   Naaman the leper dipped himself in the Jordan River three times and was cleansed of his disease *(2 Kings 5)*.

o   Joshua and the children of Israel marched around the walls of Jericho for seven days. Finally the walls fell flat and they were able to destroy the city *(Joshua 6)*.

o   Peter cast a line into the Sea of Gallilee and found money to pay his taxes in the mouth of a fish *(Matthew 17:27)* .

o   Servants at the wedding in Cana had no wine for the celebration. They filled pots with water, from which Jesus produced excellent wine *(John 2)*.

o   Isaac planted a crop in the midst of drought. That year he reaped a hundredfold harvest *(Genesis 26:12)* .

o   A widow, deeply in debt, was down to her last jar of oil. She poured her last drops of oil into borrowed pots. Miraculously, the vessels filled with oil; she was able to pay her debts and survive off the rest *(2 Kings 4)*.

o   Sick visitors at the pool of Bethesda jumped into the pool first, and were healed *(John 5)*.

o   Friends of a man who was sick with palsy carried him to the place where Jesus was and lowered him down through the roof. Jesus restored him to health *(Mark 2)*.

o   A centurion with a sick servant petitioned Jesus to speak words of healing. The servant was cured *(Matthew 8:5)*.

In each of these Bible stories, people put their faith into action. They were quick to do what they believed God wanted, to find the answers to their prayers. God responded by fulfilling His promises. Put your faith to the test; back it up with specific deeds. The results of those actions will demonstrate the soundness of your faith. Are you convinced God has a husband or wife for you, or do you simply wish it to be so? Doing something constructive and God-inspired will strengthen your faith until God's response becomes evident.

In order to start doing what God wanted me to do, I had to rid myself of all my assumptions about pursuing marriage. I had to understand that

71

God loved me and wanted to give me the desires of my heart. As I continued to pray and to counsel with my pastor, I began to see more clearly the actions I must take. The primary goal was to meet my husband before my 30th birthday, approximately six month away. I felt sure that the following steps would be pleasing to God:

1. List acceptable ways to meet men and establish godly relationships.

2. List things God does not want me to do in order to meet men.

3. Seek counsel from married Christian women on how they met their husbands. My experiences had helped me understand that "Where no counsel is, the people fall: but in the multitude of counsellors there is safety" *(Proverbs 11:14, KJV)*.

4. Break off my engagement with the devil: self-pity, envy, depression.

5. List obstacles I might find in pursuit of my goals.

6. Stay self-controlled and alert, because my enemy "the devil prowls like a roaring lion looking for someone to devour" *(1 Peter 5:8)*.

Within that framework, I set specific goals for each of the action steps.

A. *Things I will Do*

Action	Timeline
o Pray more earnestly and specifically.	Start today
o Dress attractively.	Start today
o Maintain a positive attitude and self image.	Start today
o Stay in shape: run three times a week.	Start today
o Pay off all my bills.	By my birthday
o Make a list of people to invite to the wedding.	This week
o Choose songs for the wedding.	This week
o Ask friends to serve as matchmakers for me.	Starting today
o Confess to people that I will be married soon.	This week
o Send for Christian wedding invitations. (They arrived the day I met my husband.)	Today

B. Things I Will Not Do :

o I will not date just for the sake of dating; this will delay my goal of getting married.

o I will not compromise my Christian principles by acting seductively *(Ecclesiastes 7:26)*.

o I will not give up!

o I will not date non-Christians - no missionary dating.*

*"Missionary dating" refers to situations in which Christians intentionally date unbelievers, hoping to win them over to the Lord. Avoid that trap at all costs. First, you may get involved with someone who pretends to accept the Lord in order to be with you. Second, you are likely to face much greater pressure to compromise in sexual sin. Third, the relationship is clearly in violation of God's Word, and the two of you are bound to be spiritually incompatible.

Crissy and Patrick

The story of my friend Crissy illustrates the grave dangers of missionary dating. Crissy was nearing thirty-five and wanted desperately to be married. Then she met Patrick, an attractive, charming, but unsaved young man who expressed an interest in her. She started "witnessing" to Patrick and he reponded in a positive manner. Crissy is a compassionate, sympathetic person, and Patrick soon found he could dump all his emotional baggage on her. They spent hours on the phone. Patrick began sending her flowers and asking her out for lunches and dinners.

Naturally, Crissy was flattered by all the attention. Hoping to create a spiritually compatible relationship, she convinced Patrick to start attending her church. In a moment of weakness, she had sexual intercourse with him, and became pregnant. Patrick convinced her that he loved her and wanted to marry her. Quickly and secretly, they went to a justice of the peace and got married.

Soon afterward, Patrick resumed his bad habits. He began to drink, lost several jobs as a result, and finally turned to drugs. For several years, Crissy's life was a living hell, until finally Patrick walked out for good. Today, Crissy is a single mother struggling to raise two children alone.

C. Seek Counsel from Married Christian Friends

Action	Timeline
o Make a list of friends to meet with	This week
o Develop a list of questions to ask.	Next week
o Call to set up appointments.	Next week

D. Break off my engagement with the Devil

Action	Timeline
o Develop an aggressive attitude toward the devil.	Immediately
o Identify things people say that make me feel sad	This week
o Memorize verses that speak to the situation.	Ongoing

E. Obstacles I will probably face

Obstacle	How to Deal with It
Negative friends who reinforce false assumptions about marriage.	Ignore the scoffers. Remember how people laughed as Noah built the ark.
Rejection by a specific man.	Shake off the dust, praise God, and keep going. Clearly he's not the one.

Be Convinced in Your Spirit

Jesus constantly reminded his disciples to substitute faith for doubt, emphasizing that faith alone would literally let them move mountains and cast them into the sea. It is important to understand that nothing can happen until you become unshakably convinced that it will happen, by faith. This is more than persistence, which means sticking to a cause until it succeeds. Being convinced is knowing in your innermost being that you will realize your desire for marriage. You must be assured of the REALITY of being married. You must be able to visualize yourself going for pre-marital counseling, selecting wedding attire, and standing at the altar with the one you love. As you become convinced, you will develop courage and be able to cast aside all doubt.

"...But when he asks, he must believe and not doubt, because he who doubts is like a wave of the sea, blown and tossed by the wind. That man should not think he will receive anything from the Lord; he is a double-minded man, unstable in all he does" *(James 1:6-8)*.

You must be convinced, in your heart as well as your head, that God wants you to be married. During my single years, it was sometimes easier to believe that God wanted my friends to be married and that He would provide husbands for them, than to believe He wanted that for me. I hoped and wished for a husband, but years went by and I didn't really believe in my spirit that I would get married. Not until I had studied the scriptures and said them aloud, over and over, did faith come to my heart. Meditating on those scriptures made it very clear to me that God did want me to be married, and he really had a husband for me.

Confess with Your Mouth

Proverbs 18:21 says "The tongue has the power of life and death." As part of your responsibility to work toward the answer to your prayers, you must confess with your mouth what God is doing. Your confession is crucial because of the value of "self-fulfilling prophecies."

First, base your confession not only on what you feel, see and hear, but on the truth in God's Word. Pragmatic, logical friends may accuse you of being unrealistic. What they really want you to do is acknowledge what they perceive as reality. Remember there is a spiritual reality in this life that natural man cannot see. The truth you confess is the spiritual truth and the spiritual reality of God's total world.

Secondly, only a balanced confession can be effective. A balanced confession incorporates the reality of the physical and supernatural power of God's spiritual world. Your confession acknowledges the limitations of the physical world and the overriding power of God's spiritual world.

Third, to be effective, your confession must always build yourself and others up, never tear anyone down. What you confess must be useful to you spiritually, mentally, physically and emotionally. Tell someone that you are getting married. More importantly, tell yourself--again and again--that you are getting married. Look in the mirror and assure yourself that you will soon be married.

Creative power is in the tongue. God created the heavens and earth by speaking them into existence. As you read *Genesis 1,* notice that the words "And God said" preface every creative act. For example, in *Genesis 1:3* ..."And God said, "Let there be light," and there was light." The Word of God is powerful: Jesus is "The Word" *(John 1).* There is power in what we say with our mouths. "For verily I say unto you, That whosoever shall say unto this mountain, Be thou removed, and be cast into the sea; and shall not doubt in his heart, but shall believe that those things which he saith shall come to pass; he shall have whatsoever he saith" *(Mark 11:23, KJV).*

Throughout the Bible God places great emphasis on confession. This is not just positive thinking, as some may believe. It is an essential spiritual exercise that God clearly instructs His children to engage in. In its most common usage, confession signifies the admission and acknowledgement of one's faults, mistakes and sins. The other aspect of confession, which is too often overlooked, means agreeing with, believing, and trusting what God says, and affirming the results of His Word.

For instance, when we quote *Romans 10:9* in an evangelistic context, we are in effect confessing the validity of that verse. The essence of confession is saying back to God what He has said to us. God puts His Words into our mouths, and we speak those words back to Him as our confession. "...Faith cometh by hearing, and hearing by the Word of God" *(Romans 10:17).*

Your confession must be made with utmost seriousness. For the Word of God makes it clear that the very eternal life of our souls through salvation depends upon individual confession. You simply cannot be saved without confession.

Should confession, therefore, be always verbal? The message of scripture strongly indicates that it must. In *Psalm 81:10, 11,* God tells the children of Israel "...open wide your mouth and I will fill it. But my people would not listen to me; Israel will not submit to me." God wanted to take away their slave language of hardship, discouragement, fears, and doubts, and give them the language of deliverance: His providence, His presence, His possibilities and power. But they would not listen. Because they would not confess what God wanted them to, murmuring and complaining became their confession. They paid dearly, delaying their blessing for more than forty years and losing generations in the wilderness. Faith, action and confession can work together to help you find your mate. Remind God of His Word. Stand on it.

Joseph's Story

Joseph, a friend of ours from Africa, once told us that as a student, he wanted nothing so much as to continue his education in the United States. He told all his friends about his ambition to study here. Finally he went to the U.S. Embassy to apply for a visa, but was rejected. After waiting a year to reapply, he was turned down again.

During the third year, Joseph became a Christian, and began to confess with greater assurance that God was on his side. He felt that because it was the third year of his quest, symbolizing the Trinity, he would definitely succeed. He told his parents that this would be his year to leave for the U.S. Just before his appointment at the embassy, he announced in church that the following week he would definitely get his visa and return to testify to the glory of God.

On the appointed Tuesday, armed with his passport and all the relevant documents, he walked confidently into the United States Embassy and took his place in line. When it was his turn, the consulate never glanced up, but took his passport and stamped it "DENIED." Then, looking at him firmly, she said, "Don't come back!" Joseph recalls the episode as demoralizing, depressing, and shameful. He felt like dying. He began to question whether he had really heard from God. He had set a deadline, confessed it, claimed it, believed it. Because it didn't happen in the way he wanted, at the time he believed it would happen, he was devastated.

Little by little, he recovered from his disappointment and continued to believe that God would give him a breakthrough. Whenever he was discouraged, people seemed to come out of nowhere to encourage him. Finally, years after his pilgrimage began, he was granted a visa.

Staying on God's Timetable

You may confess, "I will be married in January of next year." And suddenly it's December and no potential spouse is in sight. Don't be discouraged. Always remember that while it is important to set goals, don't etch them in concrete. When you are inflexible, you may become oblivious to new directions God is trying to give. If your plans do not come to pass as you confessed them, don't be tempted to "help" God bring the answer to your prayer on your own timetable.

There is a difference between acting on your faith and taking the initiative away from God. You will not throw your phone number at everyone who says hello. You won't begin to look at everybody as a possible mate just because you feel time is running out. If you get to the point in your confession where only a miracle can bring it to pass, don't panic. When God says it is time to act, do just what He asks you to do-- nothing more or less. Be persistent and take the kinds of constructive actions that glorify the Lord.

Trying to help God make things work may delay His plans for you. Meditate on the story of Sarah and Abraham in *Genesis 18.* Like Abraham and Sarah, you may end up creating problems even after you receive your blessing. So, if your personal deadline is passing, it doesn't mean God has overlooked you. When you begin to compromise your faith it becomes more difficult to be where God wants you at the time God wants you to be there.

One of the surest signs of Christian maturity is the willingness to give God thanks in everything--pleasant or unpleasant. Some people panic, others just become angry. "How can I face my friends? Why has God forgotten me?" Don't make excuses for God, and don't rationalize or find fault with the vision. Don't begin to say, "Maybe I was wrong." God does His work in the fullness of time.

Take a moment to complete the "Personal Goal Sheet" at the end of this chapter. It will help you focus on the specific actions you can take. Put your goal sheet where you can see it every morning and night. Do something every day to achieve your goal, and don't be discouraged. Pray and ask God how to proceed. Some people get excited when God instructs them to do something, then give up when their hopes are not fulfilled right away. Don't worry; God has perfect timing. In the fullness of time He will answer your prayers.

Chapter 4. Act on Your Prayers

Summary Review Points

1. Focus on the solution. Don't be problem-oriented.
2. Realize that God lets us participate in the answer to our prayers.
3. Do something that God directs.
4. Write down your action goals.
5. Confess with your mouth that you are getting married.
6. Prepare your personal goal sheet, using the following model.

Your Goals:

A. List things you will do, steps you will take, and a timeline for each step.

B. List things you will NOT do.

C. Counsel with married Christian friends.

      1. List people whose counsel you will seek. Set up appointments.

      2. List questions you will ask.

D. List strategies you can take against the enemy.

E. List the obstacles you may face, and how you will deal with them

---

Author's note. Please note that my goal sheet was just that--mine. The fact that it worked for me does not mean it will work in exactly the same way for you. It is not a blueprint of goals for everyone. As Jesus demonstrated throughout His ministry, God deals with each of us on an individual basis and treats us as the unique beings we are.

Chapter Five

Resist the Devil

"Resist the devil, and he will flee from you"
(James 4:7b).

During all the years I longed to be married, Satan worked hard to keep me discouraged and depressed. He filled my mind with hurtful thoughts: "What good is it to be a woman if I can't fulfill the destiny created for woman--to be a wife and mother?" "I'm horrible, useless; nobody wants me." As *Proverbs 13:12a* says, "hope deferred makes the heart sick." Sometimes I would wake early in the morning in a daze of loneliness, and stare into space. I worried about being alone for the rest of my life. Even on the remote chance that I might find a husband, I worried about giving birth to a disabled child, because I would be so old. I endured years of Satan's mental harassment.

Finally I could take it no more. One night I stood on my bed--literally on my Bible (hoping it wasn't too sacrilegious)--and literally yelled at the forces of Satan, telling them to leave me alone. I knew Satan was the only thing standing in the way, keeping my husband and me from find-ing each other. I also screamed out to God. "Lord, I'm standing on Your promises. Let God be true and every man a liar. Either this Word is true and true for me or everything that I've based my life on is a lie. You say You love me; You say You want to give me the desires of my heart; You say all I have to do is believe and act on that belief. I'm taking You at Your Word. I believe You. I'm getting married."

Following that moment of direct, intense encounter with the Lord and with the forces of darkness, I suddenly felt free, released. I received what some people refer to as rhema knowledge ("the lights clicked on").

I knew beyond a shadow of doubt that God had heard me and that I would be getting married soon. My apprehensions about the possibility of marriage turned into a calm peace and assurance. I now had a sense of expectation and anticipation that my day was coming fast.

After you've prayed and started moving toward your objective, Satan will often go on full attack to discourage you and thwart your dreams. He will attempt to destroy your peace, your joy, your efforts, and your faith. Don't give up. This is just an old trick of the devil. For children of God who know the Word, this trick of the enemy has already been uncovered. Always remember that Satan puts up his toughest fight when you are closest to your blessing.

Satan will even send counterfeits (unsaved or married people) to try to distract you when you come close to meeting the person God has for you. "For Satan himself masquerades as an angel of light. It is not surprising, then, if his servants masquerade as servants of righteousness." *(2 Corinthians 11:14,15a).*

Resolve not to fall into Satan's trap. Remember that sin and disobedience only delay your blessings and frustrate your goals. Among the other tools that the enemy may use to attack you are lies, discouragement, misinformation, opposition, disobedience, and sin. *John 10:10* says, "The thief comes only to steal and kill and destroy." You must be ready to take on the wicked powers that stand in the way of your blessings, to fight Satan and his host of demons. There is no other shortcut to your blessings. Engage in confrontation and spiritual warfare with the assurance that you will win no matter what!

God is on your side. As Hezekiah said in *2 Chronicles 32:7,* "Be strong and courageous. Do not be afraid or discouraged because of the king of Assyria (the enemy and the vast army with him) for there is a greater power with us than with him. With him is only the arm of flesh, but with us is the Lord our God to help us and to fight our battles."

The Bible teaches us that God hears our prayers from the first day we pray. He has your blessing and is ready to give it to you. But Satan is doing all he can to stand in the way and make you feel that he has been able to subvert God's plans for your life. We read in *Daniel 10:12,13* that Satan resisted Daniel. He even tried his dirty tricks on Jesus.

Why Does Satan Oppose Your Marriage?

Many singles never give much thought to the fact that Satan is actively working to prevent their marriages. But if you believe *John 10:10,* it should be clear that Satan is out to do just that. There are several biblical reasons why Satan will plot and plan against your getting married. Let's take a moment to examine some of them.

First, Satan knows that "two are better than one, because they have a good return for their work: if one falls down, his friend can help him up. But pity the man who falls and has no one to help him up! Also, if two lie down together, they will keep warm. But how can one keep warm alone? Though one may be overpowered, two can defend themselves." *(Ecclesiastes 4:9-12a).*

The truth of strength in numbers is proven over and over again through-out human experience. As *Ecclesiastes 4:12b (KJV)* says, "a three-fold cord is not quickly broken." Satan has to work much harder at attacking two people than just one. His most effective strategy, therefore, is to divide and conquer. Every time he succeeds in dividing people, he is more likely to succeed in implementing his plans. As long as Satan can keep you and your future spouse apart, he can continue to interfere with the shared destiny that God has planned for you.

Secondly, Satan knows that: "As iron sharpens iron, so one man sharp-ens another" (Proverbs 27:17). When two Christians get married and are both diligent in pursuing their relationship with the Lord, they become a dangerous force against Satan--not so much in the sense of being offen-sive or aggressive, but as a formidable defensive weapon. When such a couple maintains open, honest communication, they have absolute freedom to warn each other when Satan is trying to attack them. The stronger partner can defend the weaker one. They sharpen and protect each other against Satan's attacks.

Because Satan understands this, I honestly believe that he and his host of demons spend countless sleepless nights trying to find ways of prevent-ing or neutralizing Christian marriages.

Third, Satan knows that "one man can chase a thousand, or two put ten thousand to flight." *(Deuteronomy 32:30).* In the past, I had not given much thought to the practical application of this scripture in my day-to-day life. When I got fed up with being single and really determined that I would be married, this verse literally screamed at me. For the first time, I saw that it referred to unity of spiritual purpose, to aggressive opposition to Satan and his plans, and to the effectiveness of joining forces against Satan.

When you pray alone, a thousand demons start to flee from you. When you pray with your spouse, you send ten thousand demons fleeing. If you were in Satan's position, which would you prefer--the disorientation and nullification of one thousand or ten thousand of your agents? Satan will do everything possible to keep nine thousand demons in business against you by keeping you and your spouse apart. It is in his best interest to do so.

Of course, you do not have to be married to apply this spiritual truth for a breakthrough. Right now, team up with another single person who desires to be married as intensely as you do. Be careful about whom you select. Best of all, pray about your decision very carefully. If you have friends who are content to remain single, leave them alone. You want a prayer partner with an overwhelming desire to be married, who is honest about not wanting to remain single; someone who is not just "hoping."

Once you find such a person, schedule specific times to meet and pray together over your mutual needs. You can pray over the phone or in any other way that is convenient, but pray purposefully, aggressively, and intensively. Don't give Satan and his demons rest or peace of mind to further their sinister plans. Send them fleeing in their multitudes as you pray together.

The Importance of Family

When we study the Scriptures carefully, it is quite clear that it is the will of God that we conduct world evangelism on two fronts. On the first front, God expects Christians to raise godly children who are trained to know and obey the will and the ways of the Lord (read *Deuteronomy 4:9-10,6:7,* and *11:19,* and *2 Timothy 1:5).*

In *Malachi 2:15a,* the prophet gives us an insight into the mind of God. The verse says: "Has not the Lord made them one? In flesh and spirit they are his." Why one? Because he was seeking godly offspring. Satan understands that the population of Christians on the earth will increase as Christian couples raise children to help bring about his destruction. In fact the Lord takes this so seriously that when Eli the prophet failed in the duty of raising his children, he was rejected by God *(1 Samuel 2)*.

On the other hand, the Bible is full of examples of people who raised godly offspring unto the Lord. Esther was trained by her uncle Mordecai in the ways of the Lord. Timothy was given godly instruction by his mother and grandmother, Joseph by Isaac and Rebeccah, Isaac by Abraham and Sarah. Jesus received a godly upbringing from his earthly parents, Joseph and Mary. The passing on of righteousness within the family is as crucial an item on God's agenda as is winning the unsaved and dying world. Christian singles who treasure a life of obedience to the Lord and are devoted and dedicated to His ways, cannot have children outside of marriage.

Unbelievers, on the other hand, often have children both within and without the marriage union. They produce offspring with a greater probability of glorifying the devil and promoting his agenda. Christians working with the Holy Spirit, are enjoined to convert and train these non-Christians who are spiritually hostile to the will and the ways of the Lord, to help them know and follow Him *(Matthew 28: 19, 20)*.

When the church shies away from helping singles marry, we make things easier for the devil. If anything, Christians should be aggressively promoting marriage and helping singles find their God-given mates. Marriage is crucial for Christian single people. Every reasonable effort should be made to help fulfill the desire of those who wish to be married. Christian marriages anger Satan and bring honor to God. Having said all that, I do not want to leave the impression that single Christians are defenseless and at the mercy of Satan. Far from it! But the reasons given above are founded in scripture.

How Can You Resist Satan ?

The Bible says in *1 John 3:8*, "...The reason the Son of God appeared was to destroy the devil's work." In order words, Jesus came into this world with one purpose: to make the work of Satan ineffective, useless, and powerless to affect the lives of people, especially God's children.

Any time you see the statement "resist Satan," understand that you are to make the devil's work invalid, of no effect in your life and the other lives that touch yours.

When the demons saw Jesus *(Mark 1:24)*, the first thing they asked him was "Have you come to destroy us?" When you are a Christian, the devil knows it. He knows where you stand with God, and what you can do to him as a result. So the question is: How to resist and destroy the works of the devil?

First, we must know the Word of God. *1 Peter 3:15* says, "Always be prepared to answer everyone who asks you to give a reason for the hope that you have." When we know the truth of God's Word, Satan cannot deceive us. He must obey the truth of God's Word as we present it to him.

Secondly, we must have faith in God. As Christians, we have already taken the greatest step of faith towards God. Now we must continue to believe and trust in what God has to say, in every situation. We must deliberately decide to give God the benefit of all our doubts. "Without faith it is impossible to please God, because anyone who comes to him must believe that he exists and that he rewards those who earnestly seek him" *(Hebrews 11:6)*.

Believe deep in your inner spirit that God is on your side and that He desires to bless you with your spouse. Do not be ambivalent ot listen to those who suggest otherwise. Become so certain of your marriage blessing that you believe, act, and live as though you have it in your hand. (Read *1 Kings 18:21a, James 1:6-8, 2 Corinthians 5:17.)*

Third, we must know the devil's tricks. The Bible states *(2 Corinthians 2:11, 1 Timothy 3:7)* that Satan has snares and devices to trap us. When we are unaware of those devices we can easily fall prey to them. In my own situation, I had to battle the fear that I might never be married. When I became aggressive and resolved not to allow these devices to occupy my time and my mind, the path became much easier.

Fourth, we must put on the full armor of God every day. Life as a Christian is an ongoing spiritual battle. Every moment, waking and sleeping, we struggle with the forces of evil that try to lead us astray. *Ephesians 6:11-18* describes in detail the armor of God. For me, putting on the full armor of God is basically "living in the heavenly realm" so as not to fall prey to the tricks of the enemy. Daily prayer and study of God's Word, memorizing scripture, making confessions, avoiding evil company and communications can keep us fully armed against attacks of the enemy.

Fifth, we must always maintain a prayer mode. Prayer is the best way to demonstrate your dependence on God. Prayer keeps us in touch with Him for specific day-to-day guidance and direction. It is also important to pray for others in similar situations. "With all prayer and petition pray at all times in the Spirit, and with this in view, be on the alert with perseverance and petition for all the saints" *(Ephesians 6:11-13).* When you pray for others whose needs are similar to yours, you are doing something dear to the heart of Jesus. After all, He is constantly interceding for us.

Sixth, we must get violent with Satan. We can be certain of one thing: Satan is never passive. *1 Peter 5:8* tells us that "Your enemy the devil prowls around like a roaring lion looking for someone to devour." First this verse identifies the devil as the enemy; then it tells you that he is looking for someone to devour. You must appreciate the fact that the devil's search for victims is not a passive activity. Rather, Satan aggressively promotes his agenda. He organizes, plots, and dreams up snares and devices to thwart our blessings.

So we cannot fight him with a mealy-mouth, poor-me approach. It is a real war, and we must see it as such. We need warring attitudes and warlike language. We must make up our minds that we will not accept any contrary ideas; we will talk back to Satan, quote scriptures to him, remind him of who he is and who we are in Christ.

Every time you hear any suggestion contrary to your biblically-based expectations for a mate, talk back. Take the thought captive. Oppose Satan with violence and determination. As it says in *Matthew 11:12 (KJV),* "From the days of John the Baptist until now, the kingdom of heaven suffereth violence, and the violent take it by force." You must take your blessings by spiritual violence.

Seventh, we must take authority over Satan. In *Luke 10:19,* Jesus said, "I have given you authority to trample on snakes and scorpions and to overcome all the power of the enemy; nothing will harm you." You and I may forget that we have authority over Satan. If we maintain a right relationship with God, Satan cannot harm us.

Sometimes, when you hear testimonies, you get the impression that Satan is an overwhelming force, against which poor Christians have no defense. The opposite is true. Always remember this: in every encounter Jesus had with Satan while he was on earth, Satan never won, not even once! He lost every battle against Jesus. If this were not so, Jesus could not ask the Jews, "Which of you can point out a sin in my life?"

If this were not so, God could not have used Jesus as a sacrificial lamb for the atonement of our sins. Just as Jesus defeated the devil, He has given us power to do the same. Whether you feel it or not, the spiritual truth is that Satan is under your feet twenty-four hours a day. You can either keep him there or set him free. The choice is ours, but given what we know about Satan and his activities, why would we let go?

The experience of Daniel dramatizes the ongoing struggle between the forces of good and evil. Victories are won in the spiritual realm before they are manifested in the physical. Victories are won through active struggle, not mere passive wishing. Be on the offensive against the devil. Like Jesus *(Mark 8:33),* tell Satan, "Get thee behind me."

The children of Israel thought they would walk right in and possess the promised land, but they finally took it only through violent struggle. They were often discouraged, but as God tells us--over and over again-- never give up. The kingdom of heaven suffers violence, and violent men and women take it by force. You will face mountains and giants, but God wants you to take them on with authority.

Just as Joshua and his armies marched around the walls of Jericho, so you must march around your request and proclaim victory to God. Like David, you must go to the stream and find pebbles that can slay the giant. Focus your attention on God and His resources, not on your circumstances alone. Wear the victory of Christ, not the intimidation of Satan. Know the truth that stands, not the lie that crumbles, and when Satan confronts you, you will be convinced in your spirit that you have the upper hand. *1 John 4:4 (KJV)* tells us "Greater is he who is in you, than he that is in the world."

Chapter Five. Resist the Devil

Summary Review Points:

1. Recognize that Satan does not want you to marry, and that he will do all he can to prevent it.

2. Know the truth of God's Word.

3. Have faith in God.

4. Be alert to the tricks, snares, and devices of the devil.

5. Put on the full armor of God daily.

6. Pray without ceasing for yourself and others.

7. Resist Satan.

8. Get violent with Satan.

9. Use the authority you have over Satan.

Application Worksheet

1. How has Satan attacked you as you wait for marriage? Can you identify his strategies--the ordinary occurrences, events, and actions that depress you and make you want to give up? What are they?

_____

_____

_____

_____

_____

2. List scriptural references that can help you respond to the attacks you have listed above. Pray these verses any time you feel an attack coming on.

_____

_____

_____

_____

_____

3. Ask a trusted friend or relative to pray for you in these areas. Who will you ask--and when?

_____

_____

_____

_____

_____

Chapter Six

Maintain a Spirit of Expectancy

"Do I bring to the moment of birth and not give delivery?" says the Lord" (Isaiah 66:9).

"Guess what! I'm expecting!" We have all heard this happy announcement from a pregnant friend. When a woman who wants a child has conceived, we say she is "expecting." The expectant mother becomes increasingly excited, especially when the child inside her begins to move. Although she cannot yet see the child, she prepares for its birth by buying baby clothes, a crib and other things it will need. After nine months and much anticipation, there is fulfillment when the child is born. In the verse above from Isaiah, God promises that when the time is right, He will deliver.

What a beautiful promise! Even though Satan tries to resist the birth every step of the way, by delaying or denying fertility, or by sending complications during pregnancy and labor, God says that when you come "to the moment" of birth, you can be assured that He will deliver.

Similarly, you have a desire to be married. The seed implanted in your heart is the Word--the promise--of God. You nurture His promise with prayer and confession. You actually begin to feel in your spirit that you will be married soon. But then comes the difficult period of waiting. This waiting time should be a time of great joy and expectancy. Resist Satan and the thoughts he sends to abort your dreams. Begin to prepare for your marriage by doing the things God puts it in your heart to do. Get excited, be expectant, because you know that at the appropriate time, God will deliver His promise to you.

Farmers understand this cycle of implantation, conception, expectancy and delivery. When they plant the next season's crops, they have faith that their seeds will bear fruit. They do not worry or become depressed at the amount of time it takes to produce fruit. Why do farmers continue to believe that the seeds they plant will germinate and grow? The answer is simple. They meet three basic qualifications in advance. First, they use good seed whose potential to produce is unimpaired. Then, they plant the seed in good soil. Finally, they plant in the proper season.

Farmers know that for a good harvest, it is essential to plant only good seed. As believers, we know that the Word of God is the best seed *(Luke 8:11)*. Not only is it good, *Psalm 19:7* tells us it is "perfect." In fact throughout the Bible we see evidence that God's Word, planted in good soil, produces good fruit.

> "As the rain and the snow come down from heaven, and
> do not return to it without watering the earth and making
> it bud and flourish, so that it yields seed for the sower
> and bread for the eater, so is my word that goes out of my
> mouth: It will not return to me empty, but will
> accomplish what I desire and achieve the purpose for
> which I sent it" *(Isaiah 55:10-11)*.

Maintaining a spirit of expectancy for the one God means for you to marry means continually renewing your faith in the creative power of the good seed--God's Word. As we see in *Deuteronomy 32:47* these are "not just idle words... they are your life." Once you have resolved to hold the word of God in high esteem, you must work on the soil in which the word is planted. In *Psalms 119:9,11,* David asks an important question and provides the answer. "How can a young man keep his way pure? By living according to your Word... I have hidden your word in my heart that I might not sin against you."

Colossians 3:16 tells us to "let the word of Christ dwell in you richly." It is clear that God expects us to keep His Word in our hearts. A heart full of the Word and of faith in the Lord is good soil, in which the Word of God can produce fruit. The way we understand God and act upon His Word, our attitudes and actions, our day-to-day living--all are fueled by the core beliefs we hold in our hearts. That is why *Proverbs 4:28 (KJV)* tells us to "keep your heart with all diligence, for out of it come the issues of life."

Finally, the farmer chooses the right season to plant his seeds, so that he can also expect to harvest his crop in the right season. He does not invite disappointment by knowingly planting seeds out of season or in less than ideal conditions. Unlike earthly seeds that are affected by natural conditions, however, the Word of God is able to produce fruit in every season. God takes full responsibility for the creative power of His Word.

We have neither the capacity nor the ability to originate creative words independently of God, therefore God allows us to echo His Words. Our purpose is to hear His creative Word and reflect it back to Him. God gives us the responsibility to esteem, heed, and echo the Word as the only way of maintaining a spirit and an attitude of expectancy.

Making a List and Sticking to It

So what is the spirit of expectancy? Simply put, it is the earnest and eager anticipation that our desires will be fulfilled. Last Christmas, our children provided us with a perfect example of the spirit of expectancy. Months earlier, both Kayte, our daughter, and Joshua, our son, began asking their father and me to "tell Santa" what they wanted for Christmas. In just a few days, they compiled an amazingly long list. They hoped that Mom and Dad would provide some of the things on the list; they expected Santa to bring the rest.

At about 1:15 a.m. on Christmas morning, Kayte came into our room, climbed into our bed, and woke me with the question "Mom, is Santa here yet?" She was eager to open her gifts and see what Santa had brought her. In her excitement, she literally could not sleep. We helped her back to bed, but she was still the first to wake in the morning, with even higher levels of expectation.

That excitement also illustrated the meaning of Jesus's statement that everyone must accept the kingdom of God as a little child. Your expectations for a mate must be pure, intense, engaged, and alive, never allowed to grow lukewarm.

How to Maintain a Spirit of Expectancy

"So do not throw away your confidence; it will be richly rewarded. You need to persevere so that when you have done the will of God, you will receive what he has promised" *(Hebrews 10:35,36)*.

Hold on to the promises of God; that means waiting for answers to the specific requests you put before the Lord. Sometimes, when it seems that the prayers of other people are being answered while yours are not, it may be tempting to compromise on what you placed before the Lord. Most single people know exactly what they want in a mate, but as time passes and they see what God has given other people, they either lower or raise their standards.

Determine within yourself that you will stand firm on the promises of God. If a friend tells you about some of the qualities he or she is praying for in a mate, do not rush to add those items to your list. And when you hear other Christians declare that they are content to be single, do not be intimidated into claiming the same thing even though you feel differently. People tend to copy each other and to be swayed by every wind and doctrine. But God made you a unique individual, there is no one else in the world like you. You and your desires are unique in the eyes of God. You do not need to copy anyone. Hold on to your own dreams; God will answer you, for His own glory.

We can learn from the example of Abraham, whose first son was born to his servant Hagar. When Ishmael was born, Abraham was happy to have a son; he prayed that God would prosper Ishmael. But God had specifically promised him a son by his wife Sarah, not by Hagar. Because Ishmael was not the promise, he did not receive the blessing of Isaac. If, as you wait for your mate, you insist on settling for an Ishmael, God will not stop you. If you know what you want and are in agreement with God, don't be sidetracked, no matter what!

God Will Keep His Word

Another critical factor in maintaining a spirit of expectancy is the knowledge that God will keep His Word: "For I am watching to see that my word is fulfilled *(Jeremiah 1:12)*. Keep reminding yourself that you have based your beliefs and expectations for a mate on the Word of God. *Numbers 23:19* really says it all: "God is not a man, that he should lie, nor a son of man, that he should change his mind. Does he speak and then not act? Does he promise and not fulfill?"

Be Aware of God's Seasons

Too many of us insist upon instant gratification. We're accustomed to having everything we want, when we want it. Countless commercials preach the gospel of "get it now." We have fast food restaurants, TV and microwave dinners, fax machines, and a million more ways to do things instantly. Yet in *Ecclesiastes 3:1,* God says, "There is a time for everything, and a season for every activity under heaven."

As we saw in Chapter 2, God is very detailed about everything He does. His precision includes the patterns as well as the timing of His work. The life of Jesus offers clear evidence that God has an appointed time for everything. Jesus received a plea for help when Lazarus was sick to the point of death. But He waited three days, until after Lazarus had died, before going to him. Because the situation looked hopeless and beyond control, He achieved greater glory for God by raising Lazarus from the dead. It was such a miraculous event that no one else could possibly claim credit for it. That's the way God wants to receive His glory.

Jesus's meeting with the woman at the well demonstrated God's perfect timing. When the servant of Abraham found Rebekah at the well, God was again proving His perfect timing. The servant arrived at just the time Rebekah was there to draw water. When Moses arrived at the well where Zipporah and her sisters had gone to draw water, it was another proof of God's perfect timing.

Cornelius, another example, was a righteous man who desired a relationship with the Lord. Praying to the Lord for someone to show him how to become a Christian, he sent his servants to look for the apostle Peter. At that moment Peter, who was praying on his roof, received a vision from the Lord. God arranged the timing to help Peter change his preconceived notions about the Gentiles. The timing was so perfect that as soon as Peter received the message of God, the servants of Cornelius came to his door. Peter went with the servants; Cornelius and all his household were saved.

Innumerable examples teach us the simple lesson that God is never late, never early, always just on time. If you are at a point in your life when you want desperately to be married, and will do whatever the Lord instructs you to accomplish that goal, you are ready for God's timing.

Maintain an Open Attitude Toward God

During the last four years, two of my good friends have married. I believe it was because they had reached a new heightened expectancy toward finding their mates. In both cases, the circumstances were very interesting. Their blessings in finding their mates illustrate an important point. God will guide you in the right direction if you seek His will and act on your faith.

Barry is a friendly, outgoing, down-to-earth person. He has been very active in our church, and is fully committed to the Lord. Most people seem to love Barry the first time they meet him. Over the years, three of my friends--Samantha (Sam), Eileen, and Kelly--each confided to me individually that they were convinced Barry was to be their mate.

Along with a handsome appearance and a wonderful singing voice, Barry is kind and generous, with a reputation for literally giving people "the shirt off his back." So even though he had not expressed interest in any of my three friends, each was convinced that he was to be her mate.

Without saying anything to Barry or aggressively pursuing him, both Sam and Eileen told me that they were tired of being single. They were both determined to be married within two or three years. They each started praying fervently and asking God to lead them to their mates, whether it was Barry or not. Sometimes, Eileen would call me to talk and pray with her.

Within a few months after Sam began praying so earnestly, Bob, a young man who sang in the choir with her, became interested. They were soon engaged. After months of counseling and preparation, Bob and Sam were married.

Eileen also started to pray for a mate. At first Joseph, another member of our church, seemed very much interested in her. Nothing much came of it, but Eileen was not disappointed. She just kept praying and believing. Then suddenly, Kurt, a very quiet and reserved young man in our church, began to show an interest in Eileen. In less than eighteen months, Kurt and Eileen too were married.

And what about Kelly? She is in her early forties and has known Barry since he first came to the church, more than ten years ago. They served together in the choir and in several ministries, attended the same Bible study and prayer groups, and grew to be good friends. According to Kelly, Barry was always completely honest with her, telling her repeatedly that he only considered her a good friend and Sister in the Lord. But it is quite obvious to anyone who knows them that Kelly would do anything to be near Barry. She is so firmly convinced that Barry will be her husband that she has discouraged other Christian men who show an interest in her. Last year, Barry transferred to another state. Kelly has not expressed any plans to look for a new job closer to Barry, but no one would be surprised if she did. Meanwhile, she is renting Barry's house. She is still single, and still sure that he will be her husband.

Is Kelly wrong in her expectations? No, since Barry is still single, and still in touch, it's very possible that God will bring them together and prove that Kelly was right to wait for him. Ultimately, however, Kelly needs to determine whether the Lord has indeed told her that Barry will become her husband. Once she makes that determination, then she must decide whether she is willing to wait for Barry, or settle for an Ishmael *(Genesis 16-18)*.

It is interesting to note that both Sam and Eileen were both married within the two- to three-year period of their prayers. At this point, you may be saying "Now, wait a minute. I don't know about this business of giving God a deadline when He must answer my prayer and give me my husband or wife."

You may be justified in your concern, but God is neither threatened nor bound by anyone's deadlines. Additionally, I do not believe He loses sleep over the idea that one of His children has a timetable for getting married. The simple fact is this: if three years had gone by and Sam and Eileen were still unmarried, it would have been obvious that their timeline did not conform to the will of God.

The Bible gives us several examples of people who needed an answer to prayer within a specific time frame, and God responded in time. When Meshach, Shadrach, and Abednego were in danger of defiling themselves with the king's food, Daniel told the king's butler to serve them vegetables and water. If they had not proven themselves worthy during that specific period, then they would have been obligated to go on the king's diet *(Daniel 1)*.

Here, in effect, is what the story signifies. God had thirty days to let the three Hebrew boys prosper as well or better on a vegetable diet than they would have done on the king's regimen. God was not threatened, but He responded. At the end of the thirty days, the boys were healthier than those who had eaten from the king's table. God respected the deadline and responded in time. So go ahead, take steps of faith. Let God direct you.

Chapter Six.
Maintain a Spirit of Expectancy

Summary Review Points

1. Understand that the Word of God is a perfect seed.
2. Hold on to the promises of God; your life depends on it.
3. Be assured that God will keep His Word.
4. Be aware of God's seasons.
5. Maintain an open attitude toward God.

Application Worksheet

1. Every morning make a confession of faith of what you are expecting God to do. *(Romans 10:17)* Write your confession here. Repeat it as often as you need to etch it permanently in your spirit. Be consistent with your confession. Don't say one thing one day and something else the next.

    _____

    _____

    _____

    _____

    _____

    _____

2. It may help you maintain your expectancy if you write your confession, with scripture verses, on index cards. Post them on your mirrors, your refrigerator door, the steering wheel of your car, etc.

3. Anticipate God's blessing each day.

Chapter Seven

Recognize the Answer

"The Lord has done this and it is marvelous in our eyes"
(Psalm 118:23).

As Christians, we see the Bible as our guide for life. The Word of God is the same yesterday, today and forever. What was good advice for Christian singles in biblical times is good advice for us now. God's Word does not change. Its pages hold instruction for every aspect of our lives, and certainly for an issue as important as finding a life partner.

How Did Men and Women in the Bible Meet Their Mates?

Let's look at some accounts of how couples from the Bible found each other for marriage. In the story of Adam and Eve *(Genesis 2:18-23),* it was God who decided that Adam needed a wife. He made Eve from Adam's rib while Adam slept. God brought the two of them together; no personal choice was involved.

In *Genesis 21:21,* Hagar, Ishmael's mother, found a wife for him in Egypt while they were living in the Desert of Paran.

In *Genesis 24,* Abraham took the initiative to provide a wife for his son Isaac. He commissioned his servant to seek a young woman for Isaac from among Abraham's own people, assuring the servant that God would send an angel to help him find the right one. The servant found Rebekah at the well, filling her pitcher. He knew she was the right woman when she gave the correct response to his question and met all of Abraham's other criteria. Rebekah agreed to go with the servant. Isaac took Rebekah as his wife, and he loved her.

Jacob's parents, Rebekah and Isaac, sent Jacob to Paddan Aram, commanding him to marry one of the daughters of Laban. *Genesis 28:7* says "Jacob obeyed his father and mother." He arrived in the land, inquired about Laban, and immediately met Rachel, at work with her father's sheep. Jacob stayed with Laban's family for a month, fell in love with Rachel and asked Laban for her hand. The text adds that Rachel was "lovely in form and beautiful." Although Jacob worked for Laban for seven years before they were married, the Bible says those years seemed like "only a few days to him because of his love for her."

When Ruth's husband died, she followed her mother-in-law, Naomi, to Bethlehem. Naomi took the initiative to help Ruth find a new husband *(Ruth 3:1-11)*. She gave Ruth specific instructions for attracting the attention of Boaz, a wealthy relative. Ruth responded, "I will do whatever you say," and "did everything her mother-in-law told her to do." Ruth worked in Boaz's fields until he noticed her and was attracted to "her noble character, and her fidelity and loyalty to her mother-in-law Naomi." Finally, as Naomi had planned, Boaz and Ruth were married.

Abigail served as mediator between David and her evil husband Nabal *(1 Samuel 25)*. Samuel also tells us that Abigail was intelligent and beautiful, and David was impressed by her good judgment and sound advice. Later, hearing of Nabal's death, David sent his servants to bring Abigail back to be his wife.

Esther, an orphan, was reared by her cousin Mordecai *(Esther 2)*. When she was a young woman, King Ahasuerus issued an edict to his people, searching for beautiful young virgins from whom to choose a bride, so Mordecai took Esther to the king's palace. Her wisdom and beauty won favor with the king, and Esther became his wife.

Many of these biblical examples have common threads. In the stories, parents or surrogate parents take the initiative to find wives or husbands for their children. In *Jeremiah 29:6,* God instructs fathers to "find wives for your sons and give your daughters in marriage." Thus, God created a wife for Adam. Abraham found a wife for his son Isaac; Hagar found a wife for Ishmael; Jethro found a husband for his daughter. Rebekah and Isaac took the initiative in providing a wife for their son Jacob. Naomi, the mother-in-law, played matchmaker for Ruth and Boaz. And Mordecai, Esther's adopted father, directed her steps toward marriage.

Even though not every case in the Bible indicates parents involved in finding mates for their children, parental approval and blessing of the marriage seems to have been the norm. In most of the examples, the parents were concerned that their children find someone from among their own people--in other words, not to marry pagans. In these examples, God demonstrates parental involvement as a biblical pattern or principle for initiating the marriage process.

In my own case, my mother told me time and again that she was praying for God to send me the right husband. I believe her prayers helped guide me to the right man. But what about people who do not have godly Christian parents or whose parents are not living? In such a case, you might ask your pastor or an older, spiritually mature couple from your church to stand in as parental figures for you. *Psalm 1:1* says, "Blessed is the man who does not walk in the counsel of the wicked" ("or ungodly"--*KJV). "* Christian surrogate parents should be able to provide prayerful support for you as you seek marriage.

Another biblical direction in regard to marriage is that the man should pursue and woo the woman. *Proverbs 18:22* says the man must go find his wife. In one important spiritual example, we see it is Christ (the groom) who woos the people of His Church (the bride) to Himself. He seeks after us; not the other way around. But while it is clearly the man's responsibility to woo and pursue, there is much that a woman can do to help him find her. Beyond the principal requirement of spiritual compatibility, from biblical times to the present day, certain characteristics tend to attract a man to a woman. Those qualities include beauty, intelligence, industry, good advice and good judgment, fidelity and family loyalty, an attitude of learning and humility.

This is by no means a complete list. You may find, once you meet your mate, other characteristics that seem more important. Take time to identify the traits you find attractive in other people, and those that other people find attractive in you. Pray that God will send you a mate who is searching for someone with your particular characteristics. It never helps to shift into "poor me" gear, making comments like "I'm no beauty, and I'm not intelligent." In most biblical examples, those qualities had little to do with the mutual attraction of the two people. It was rare for husbands to meet their wives ahead of time or propose to them in person.

Dating and the Bible

At this point, let's examine the subject of dating. When non-Christians talk about dating, they usually mean more than a platonic period during which to explore the possibility of marriage. Young people are very vulnerable and easily tempted when they spend a lot of time alone together, and dating may lead a Christian couple into sin. God is adamantly opposed to premarital sex. He tells us in *1 Corinthians 6:18* to "flee from sexual immorality."

Did couples in the Bible "date" prior to marriage? Did they find their mates at singles bars or singles church fellowships? One reason for dating is that it gives couples a chance to get better acquainted. But as experience proves again and again, people are often on their best behavior during the dating process, then revert to their "real selves" after marriage.

Nowhere in the Bible do we have any evidence of people dating. In each case, when God brought people together, they knew and acted upon it in their spirits. Try to imagine Adam and Eve dating, or Isaac and Rebekah, or Abigail and David. Dating basically is an invention of western civilization that has become associated with the process of finding a mate. But it has no biblical foundation, and thus Christians need not feel bound by it. God is able to bring your wife or husband to you without involving the dating process.

Dating may be problematic, but genuine courtship is not. The courtship process involves some level of commitment, while dating works on the basis of "trial and error." The goal of courtship is marriage. You may argue that dating often leads to courtship and marriage, and therefore is also important. This is a good argument, and if you feel you have time to spend on relationships that may lead to courtship, go ahead and date. The fact is that the result of dating is more likely to be wasted time and heartache than marriage.

If on the other hand, your primary goal is marriage, then honesty is likely to serve you better. Look for a serious courting relationship right from the start. You have a lifetime to get to know your mate. Skipping the dating period will not put you at a disadvantage.

Although singles should probably not waste time in "trial and error" dating, couples thinking about marriage should seek extensive premarital counselling through their churches. Counselling involves serious discussions with a spiritually minded, objective person who can help the couple lay a good foundation for their marriage. (See *Proverbs 11:14).*

What about "love at first sight" or "falling in love"? There seems to be no biblical basis for such an idea. Marriage is first and foremost a spiritual commitment. Marriages often break up because they are based on emotional or physical attraction rather than the spiritual foundation that God intended. Of course love is important in a marriage relationship. But love must grow out of commitment.

In actuality what most people call "love at first sight" is little more than lust. In too many cases, this so-called "love" fades when the novelty of the attraction wears off. Occasionally we find people who claim to have fallen in love at first sight, and whose marriages actually work. But in most cases, marriages founded on anything other than spiritual commitment stand on shaky ground.

The sad part is that so many Christians buy into this worldly idea, and suffer through the same problems that plague other couples. Rather than looking for godly men or women, Christian singles may focus on the physical appearance, job, income, education, natural talents and abilities of a potential mate. Of course these things are important, but they should not be the sole criteria for finding suitable mates.

God knows that we are always likely to be short-changed when "...man looks at the outward appearance" *(1 Samuel 16:7b).* God looks at the heart; He tells us in *2 Corinthians 5:16a* that "Henceforth know we no man after the flesh." In effect, He is instructing Christians to be more concerned with spirituality than external characteristics.

One primary goal in praying for a mate is to find someone genuinely committed to the Lord, someone who understands the spiritual commitment of marriage. Avoid the temptation to become so fixated on outward appearances that you end up overlooking or despising the blessings of God. The bottom line for any blessing from God, whether it is a mate or anything else, is that He knows what is best for us. He will not send you a mate whom you cannot love.

The Story of Bryan and Karen

Bryan was a security guard in the parking lot of a high-rise office building. He took a lot of pride in his work, always neatly dressed and cordial, greeting the people who parked in the lot. Bryan had been a good student, and wanted very much to go to college, but his father died while he was in high school. Bryan had to drop out before graduation to help his mother support the family. But he was constantly reading books and newspapers, trying to improve himself and extend his education.

Karen was a Certified Public Accountant and a member of Bryan's church. She worked in the building and parked her car every day in Bryan's lot. Although they attended the same church, Bryan and Karen barely knew each other.

Years went by with the two of them exchanging no more than a few casual words every day. But strangely, Bryan began to feel that Karen was the woman God wanted him to marry. Deeply aware of the differences in their educational and financial backgrounds, he was reluctant at first to give his feelings more than passing thought. But try as he might, his interest would not go away. After much prayer, and without talking to Karen, he decided to talk to his pastor about it. The pastor prayed with Bryan, and together asked God to give him an answer. The pastor also told Bryan to pray that God would reveal His truth to Karen.

Until the time Bryan began his campaign of prayer, Karen had never thought of him as a potential husband. Suddenly she found herself thinking about him more and more often. Over a period of several months, she thought about Bryan almost every day. At first, she thought it was only lust, but she became certain that the attraction was to his spirit. Although he was not outstandingly attractive, increasingly she found herself thinking about Bryan as a husband.

She too went to talk to the pastor about her feelings. She told the pastor, "When I get to the 15th floor of my office building, I find myself gazing down out of the window, looking for him." She also told the pastor that she was uncomfortable with the idea of becoming involved with someone who was only a security guard with little formal education. The pastor counselled her that if God intended to bring them together, He would make things work for them.

At the pastor's suggestion, each began praying that God would tell the other. Finally Bryan summoned enough courage to tell Karen about his feelings. He suggested that they meet with their pastor to discuss the differences in their backgrounds. Bryan said, "Even though I want to do God's will, I'm concerned. Karen is so well educated, and I'm not. It would be very difficult for me to catch up." He began to study at home.

After months of counseling, Bryan and Karen were married. He took the high school equivalency exam and passed. He applied for and was admitted to a local college. Karen encouraged him to go to a Bible college instead, since he had always felt called to the ministry. Today, Bryan is a minister and Karen is very proud to be his wife.

Listen to the Holy Spirit

Bryan and Karen are examples of singles who found peace in their choice of mates, because God took the initiative in showing them who to marry. They both listened to the voice of the Holy Spirit; both wanted what God wanted for their lives. On the other hand, I know single people who become so fixated on what their eyes can see that they overlook the mate God has for them.

What about "naming and claiming" a husband or wife? Is it a biblical idea? In this era of positive thinking, people seem to believe that they can name and claim just about anything mentioned in the Word of God. Unfortunately, in their eagerness to get what may be coming to them, people fail to understand that some of God's promises are conditional.

Even in my circle of friends, I know single people who feel strongly that God wants them to marry a certain Christian person in the church. They may have prayed for years and years without results; in each case, the objects of those prayers were totally uninterested. My friends have "named and claimed" their future mates, which means they believe God has revealed the one they are to marry through a dream or prophecy or word of knowledge. They believe if they have enough faith, eventually the chosen one will turn to them. Unfortunately, as the years go by, the "intended" often marries someone else.

If you find yourself in that kind of situation, first of all evaluate your convictions honestly. Are they really from God? Basically, if God gives you a revelation He will be faithful in bringing it to pass. As the Bible says, "God is watchful over His Word to perform it." It is also possible that your future mate does not yet have the same revelation. In such a situation you need to refocus your prayer in the following direction.

o   Ask God for additional confirmation that this is the person He means for you to marry. Study Gideon *(Judges 6:36-40)* to learn how he sought confirmation from the Lord.

o   Ask God to reveal to you whether your heart is deceiving you. *(Jeremiah 17:9)*.

Make sure to resolve these two issues in your spirit, not just in your mind, before you proceed to the next step. Then:

o   Pray that God will change the heart of this person toward you. "The heart of the king is in the hand of the Lord" *(Proverbs 21:1)*.

o   Pray that the Spirit of God will reveal to your chosen one that you are the mate He intends, and that he or she accepts that revelation.

Studying the stories of couples in the Bible, we see that God willed them to marry in order to accomplish His divine eternal purposes. I believe that God will put you and your mate together to accomplish a specific intention for his kingdom. God wants you and your mate to bring glory to Him and to His kingdom, as in the following examples.

o   Eve was created to be a helpmeet for Adam.

o   Jacob and Rachel were to have children who would "become a community of peoples... who would take possession of the land God gave to Abraham" *(Genesis 28:3)*.

o   The offspring of Ruth and Boaz were to build the house of Israel *(Ruth 4:11)*.

o   Abigail helped David avert the danger of Nabal's folly *(Genesis 25)*.

o   Esther was called to her position as the king's wife to save her people, the Jews, whom Haman would have killed *(Esther 2-8)*.

Knowing When It's Right

After years of waiting and praying, I finally met my husband-to-be, Ben, in a way I never would have expected. After Ben graduated from college, he worked in Chicago for a year. He had been accepted into a graduate program in Texas on a partial scholarship, but needed to work for a while to raise the rest of his tuition.

He arranged to stay with his friend, Arthur, in Baltimore and look for a summer job there. When Ben arrived in Baltimore, he called Arthur to pick him up or give him directions to the apartment. But Arthur told him regretfully that his roommate had changed his mind and did not want a third person to stay in the apartment. With no place to stay, Ben had to find his own accommodations in Baltimore for the summer. He also started looking for a job in his field, without much success.

Just as he had run out of money, he found a job with a construction company. There Ben met Harold, a co-worker in his 50's, and started attending his church. Ben developed a close relationship with the pastor and learned that the church had an apartment available for rent. He and Harold decided to share the apartment.

Meanwhile, my goal that year was to meet my future husband before my birthday in August. As summer drew near, I grew more expectant, yet I felt strongly that I had to do something to meet this man. Finally, after struggling with this somewhat unconventional idea, I decided to place a "personals" ad in a respectable magazine in town. My best friend, Joy, supported the idea and even agreed to share the ad with me. In my wildest imagination I never thought I would be placing such an ad; it seemed completely out of character for me. Somehow, though, I felt strongly that I had to make this last-ditch effort to find my mate. After much discussion and prayer, Joy and I wrote our ad:

> "Two Christian single females, both 29, in search of two
> professional single men, 29 to 35, who love the Lord.
> We're attractive professionals, enjoy running, sports,
> theater, travel. Please reply with friend or singly."

Over the next few weeks, we received mail responses from a lot of people who were clearly not the ones God had in mind for us. Some were Christians, and others definitely were not, but not one was the man of our prayers.

Meanwhile, Ben and Harold had become very good friends. They spent a lot of time together--cooking and eating meals together, and spending hours in the libraries reading. They became like father and son. For some reason, Harold began to encourage Ben very strongly to get married. To this day, Ben is not sure why Harold was so adamant. Ben maintained that he was not ready for marriage, that his immediate goal was to finish graduate school, but Harold persisted. He suggested that Ben look through the "personals" ads in a few magazines, but Ben was not interested.

One day Harold brought home a magazine that happened to have the ad Joy and I had written. Somehow this magazine had reprinted our ad-- without our permission--from the magazine where we had placed it. Only God knows how that happened, but Harold was immediately drawn to our ad. He pointed it out to Ben, who read it and threw it away. For more than a month, Harold nagged Ben to respond to the ad. Finally, he agreed to write, thinking nothing would come of it. He drafted a letter and kept it for more than two weeks. Then, at Harold's constant urging, he rewrote and mailed it.

Joy picked up Ben's letter from our post office box. As soon as she read it, she knew it was not for her, but for me. Reading Ben's letter, I knew immediately that this one was different, this one was important. When I wrote back and he responded in French, I knew he was the one.

The events that brought us together proved to Ben and me that life is not just a series of random events. Rather, God's pattern of interconnected, skillfully designed pieces, tend to form a "big quilt." The Bible says in *Romans 8:28 (KJV)* "And we know that all things work together for good to them who love God, to them who are called according to his purpose." Our experience proved to me beyond a shadow of doubt that God's way is always the best. Ben and I probably never would have met without a lot of seemingly unrelated events:

o   If Ben had gone straight from Chicago to graduate school, he would never have gone to Baltimore.

o   If Arthur's roommate had agreed to let Ben stay for the summer, he and Harold would not have become such good friends.

o   If Ben had found a job in his field--accounting--he would not have sought construction work, and if God had not provided that specific job, he would probably never have met Harold.

o   If Joy and I had been too reluctant to place the personals ad, and if our ad had not been mysteriously reprinted in the second magazine, Harold and Ben might never have found it.

So although Ben was initially disappointed with the events of that summer, it was all the Lord's hand at work. That series of events illustrates what Joseph meant when he said to his brothers, "You intended to harm me, but God intended it for good, to accomplish what is now being done" *(Genesis 50:20).* God knows how to use any circumstance, no matter how difficult, to bring about his purposes for our good. Most often, in the midst of the storm, we do not see or understand God's purposes. But if we keep believing, God always shows himself faithful.

After several phone conversations, Ben and I arranged to meet at a French restaurant. Remembering my prayer request for a mate who could speak French, I was thrilled to hear him place our orders in fluent French. But then, Ben seemed to answer all of my prayers. One of the things I had prayed about was the age of my future husband--about my age, not older than thirty-six. It turned out that Ben was exactly nine days older than I. What a precise God we have! He is 5 feet 6 inches tall, has a college degree, is intelligent, friendly, affectionate, articulate, and well-groomed. He is a hard worker and loves to travel. Most important of all, Ben is a mature, believing Christian.

All of these details demonstrate the importance of being very specific in your prayers for a husband or wife, so you will know for a certainty when the right one comes along. During our first phone conversation Ben mentioned that he had been saved since July 1979, and had been Spirit-filled around the same time. He shared his testimony with enthusiasm, and told me about all the summers he spent as a counselor in Christian camps. He mentioned that he had been involved with the Navigators (a campus ministry) for several years. I never had any doubt of his intimate relationship with the Lord.

Because of his association with the Navigators, Ben regularly memorizes Scripture, shares his faith, and leads other people to the Lord. In fact, when we met he had already started teaching a children's Bible class at

111

the church he and Harold attended. I was amazed at the frequency and the fervency of his prayer life. Ben prayed about everything and everyone. Even on our strolls around the city, Ben would often pause to pray. Over the eight years of our marriage, Ben has proven to be a true and consistent prayer warrior.

Not only did he meet all my criteria, we found we had many additional things in common. For example, we both loved Keith Green and his ministry through music, restaurants, reading, and running. I was convinced in my spirit that God had sent Ben to me. Clearly, when you are specific in your prayers for a husband or wife, you know with certainty when the right person comes along.

How did Ben know that I was to become his bride? In college, he had interviewed more than two hundred Christian couples about how they had recognized their mates. Many couples said they knew by the inner peace and unconditional love that they felt for their partners. For the next six years, Ben had prayed that God would give him complete peace and unconditional love for his future wife from the first time he met her. During those six years, he met a number of lovely Christian women, some of whom wanted to marry him. But he never felt the inner peace and unconditional love he was seeking. From the moment we met, Ben told me later, he felt his prayers for love and peace were answered.

Ben and I went through months of pre-marital counseling at my church, and Ben also had counselling with his pastor. We married six months after we met. We have been happily married for eight years and have two beautiful children. I never imagined God would send such a wonderful answer to my prayers. Not only did He grant me my petition for a husband, He gave me much more.

> "(God) is able to do immeasurably more than all we ask or imagine, according to his power that is at work within us..." *(Ephesians 3:20).*

Howard and Joy, Linda and Gerald

Meanwhile, although I had finally met Ben, my friend Joy had not yet found anyone. Joy and I were very special friends. We had asked the Lord not to let either of us marry and leave the other alone; we could not bear the thought of one of us experiencing the joy of being married while the other remained single. As happy as I was with Ben, I continued to pray fervently that God would also send Joy's mate.

One Sunday, Ben and I went to his church together. Noticing a young man seated nearby, I felt strongly in my spirit that he might be Joy's future husband. After the service, I mentioned my feelings to Ben and he told me Howard was a good friend of his. We invited Howard out for bowling and ice cream, and to meet Joy, and before long, Joy and Howard announced their engagement. They were married one month after Ben and me, and have also been happily together for eight years. They and their son are currently living in Germany.

God also used Ben and me to bring together another couple in our church. Linda was in the same ministry I was. She had been engaged for some time, on and off, to marry David. It was a rocky engagement, with David calling it off one day and wanting to restore it the next. His excuse was that he wasn't really sure he wanted to be married. All that uncertainty caused tremendous stress for Linda. After about the third or fourth breakup and reconciliation, along with major disagreements, Linda called one night to talk to me.

Ben happened to pick up the phone, and he and Linda talked for some time. Ben suggested they pray together about her problem. As they were praying, Ben had a very strong sense that God wanted him to tell Linda to fast. He asked her to fast on the following Wednesday, about a week after the day of their conversation. She was to ask the Lord for a specific, final resolution of her situation.

On that Wednesday, while Linda was fasting, God arranged for her and David, her fiance, to do some volunteer work at the church. Peggy, our church administrator, knew that David and Linda were having problems, and she had been praying for them. Without any prior planning, Peggy decided to take David and Linda together into a room and talk to them at length about their engagement. Finally, she recommended that they break it off, once and for all.

Oddly, Linda felt tremendous peace. Because she had dedicated that particular day to seek God's will for her relationship, she felt sure that Peggy's advice was the Lord's doing. David, on the other hand, was angry at what he saw as Peggy's unjustified and unsolicited interference in his life. A week or so later, however, he admitted that he really was not ready for marriage. Linda later told me that she had become tired of David's wavering and had given the engagement ring back to him the Sunday after she talked with Ben. She had been dating David for two and half years, so even though she felt relieved, she was also heartsick at the end of that relationship.

Shortly after her engagement ended, she became more determined than ever to find her true husband. She made a list of qualities she wanted in her mate. She even called a member of her former church in Kentucky to join her in prayer. My own experience had given me tremendous empathy with other single women. I prayed for Linda several times after the breakup of her engagement. One evening, as I was praying for Linda, the Lord put it into my heart to introduce her to another friend, Gerald. I mentioned the idea to Ben. Ben agreed and suggested that we invite them to dinner after church.

When I called to tell Linda about our plans, she was amazed. She told me she had been hoping we would introduce her to someone; the idea had come to her "out of the clear blue sky" during a Mother's day dinner with her family. It was such a strong impulse that she had pinched herself and asked, "Where in the world did that come from?" All the following day she had felt she should call us, and although she decided not to, the nagging feeling would not go away. All of this had happened just before I called her to tell her of our plans.

Ben invited Gerald over for dinner after church the next Sunday. He made it clear that the primary reason for the invitation was to introduce him to Linda. That Sunday, we had an enjoyable dinner and conversation, but neither Linda nor Gerald showed more than polite interest in each other. Talking to Ben later, Gerald commented that although he thought Linda was a beautiful sister in the Lord, she was not his type. Linda also felt that nothing special would come of their meeting.

A few weeks later, however, as Linda was browsing in our church bookstore, she bumped into Gerald. He was buying a book called *Intimacy with God.* It startled her, because she had been praying for a long time that God would give her a husband who wanted, more than anything, to be "intimate with God."

114

Right there in the bookstore, Gerald asked Linda for her phone number, and they began to see each other more often. Somehow, both began to feel that God had drawn them together. About two months after their meeting in the bookstore, Gerald and Linda were engaged. That was in July of 1985. They were married a year later. Ben was in their wedding. Today Gerald and Linda have been happily married for six years and have three lovely children.

God is no respecter of persons. He wants to give you the desires of your heart, to fulfill your dreams. He will not let you err in choosing your mate if you are sincerely seeking His perfect will for your life partner.

Making Things Right

Everyone makes honest mistakes, but God has a way of rectifying those mistakes and making all things work together for good. Many people who make mistakes become disheartened and disillusioned, and take a long time to recover. They end up delaying God's blessings and the fulfillment of His promises in their life. We all make mistakes. When you make yours, confess it, pray about it and keep going.

How can you be sure you have found the right person?

1. He or she should meet the criteria on your prayer list. If you have prayed about your list and followed God's guidance to weed out any criteria that are inappropriate, God will be faithful to send you the one who meets your description. In my own case, the man God sent to be my husband met every item on my list except one--a master's degree--and I had already identified that as not really essential.

2. God will provide confirmation. "In the mouth of two or three witnesses shall every word be established" *(2 Corinthians 13:1)*. *Genesis 24* lists a number of ways that helped Isaac recognize Rebekah as the woman God meant for him. When the servant found Rebekah *(verse 21)*, "without saying a word, [he] watched her closely to learn whether or not the Lord had made his journey successful."

   a. The woman would not be one of the Canaanites with whom Abraham was living, but would come from his own country and his own people *(verses 3,4)*. In verse 15, Rebekah confirms that condition as she tells the servant that she is the daughter of

Bethuel, son of Milcah, the wife of Abraham's brother Nahor.

b. An angel was to lead the servant to the woman *(verse 7)*. That confirmation comes in *verse 27* when the servant says, "Praise be to the Lord, the God of my master Abraham, who has not abandoned his kindness and faithfulness to my master. As for me, the Lord has led me on the journey to the house of my master's relatives."

c. The servant asked God to lead him to the woman he was seeking on a particular day *(verse 12)*, confirmed in *verse 15,* "...before he had finished praying, Rebekah came out with her jar on her shoulder."

d. God assured the servant that Rebekah was the right woman. He had asked God to have her make a specific statement as they stood beside a spring, "Drink, and I'll water your camels too" in response to his request, "Please let down your jar that I may have a drink."

Following God's Clues

In my own case, not only did my husband-to-be meet all of my important criteria, God gave me other evidence that he was the one:

a. As a teenager, I once had a vivid dream and recorded it in my prayer diary. In the dream my mother was sewing robes for all the members of my family. The robes were red, white, and blue like the American flag. I did not want to wear the same colors as the rest of my family; I asked my mother to make my robe like that of another country. Can you believe that two decades later that dream was revealed to me again when my husband-to-be turned out to be from the country I had dreamed about?

b. Even though it was not on my prayer list, God seemed to be showing me that my husband-to-be would bring me a dozen roses on our first date. I kept the idea to myself and never mentioned it to Ben or anyone else. Sure enough, he showed up at the restaurant for our first meeting with 12 long-stemmed roses. Ben told me later that on his way to meet me, he had a strong urge to stop and buy roses. He had not planned on it, was not even thinking about it, but felt compelled to do so.

c. We attended church together the first Sunday after we met at the restaurant. What a surprise when the preacher announced the title of his sermon: "This is Just the Beginning." Certainly it was the beginning of our life together.

d. Friends who saw me sitting with Ben in church told me later that they were sure he was to become my husband.

e. Much earlier, I had ordered a catalog of Christian wedding invitations; it arrived on the day I met Ben.

f. My prayer to meet my husband-to-be before my birthday was answered when I met him exactly three weeks before.

g. My parents and my entire extended family totally accepted Ben and welcomed him into the family with open arms.

3. You and your mate will agree on basic Christian doctrines. Not only must you both be Christians, but the Bible stresses the importance of spiritual agreement. That biblical admonition is fundamental to the health of any marriage because it limits the ground upon which Satan can cause division between you. As Jesus said in *Mark 3:25,* "If a house is divided against itself, that house cannot stand."

Ben told me emphatically that he was not interested in dating. He said he had been praying specifically for his future wife and did not want to waste my time or his. He wanted to know right from the start my stand on a number of Christian issues he considered absolutely critical. So during our first meeting and through subsequent conversations, he asked me all the questions listed at the end of this chapter. They may be helpful to you as a way to explore the beliefs of a potential spouse.

4. You will experience unconditional acceptance for your mate. All of us enter marriage with flaws and idiosyncracies. Those who do not love and accept us for who we are can find these intolerable. It is fruitless to go into a marriage relationship with the goal of changing one's spouse. So the wisest thing to do is to ask God to give you unconditional love for each other, just as He loves us unconditionally. As *Romans 5:8* puts it, "But God demonstrates His own love toward us, in that while we were yet sinners, Christ died for us."

5. God will open doors for you. In our case, this happened quite literally. On the day Ben and I went to buy our engagement ring, we

returned to the car to discover the keys locked inside. We tested the doors and they were all locked. We decided not to panic, but rather to pray. After praying we were astonished to see that one lock had miraculously slid over to the open position.

We interpreted it as God's way of showing us that He would continue to open doors for us in our relationship. From that moment, He has done just that. For example, when we needed money for wedding expenses, God sent Ben both full-time and part-time accounting jobs. As you face challenging situations together, you will see the evidence of God's hand at work.

Of course this discussion can only suggest a few ways you might recognize your mate. Each individual is unique, and God has unique ways of dealing with us and answering our prayers. You are welcome to use these items as general guidelines, but keep your spirit open to God's specific direction for your life. When you have an open attitude, you can appreciate the verse "I will...shew thee great and mighty things which thou knowest not" *(Jeremiah 33:3, KJV)*.

Ben's Questions

Ben asked me a series of questions on our first date. Over the next few weeks, we discussed additional questions face-to-face and on the phone. Ben told me he had devoted a lot of thought and prayer to these questions. He knew he could not enter any relationship without first having answers--through direct response and careful observation.

Be sure to read them all. They may help you create your own list of vital questions as you journey toward marriage.

1. Do you believe the whole Bible as the divine Word of God?

2. Are you a born again Christian believer? For how long?

3. Could you briefly share your testimony about how you came to know the Lord?

4. How serious would you say you are with your Christian life and how do you demonstrate that seriousness?

5. What would you say is the most meaningful change in your life since you became a Christian?

6. How often do you share your faith and witness to people about Jesus?

7. Would you want your future family to witness as a regular part of its weekly activities?

8. Do you have regular Quiet Times alone with God? When, how often, and why?

9. Would you want to share Quiet Times with your future partner?

10. Approximately how many people would you say have come to know the Lord through you?

11. What are your favorite verses in the Bible? Why?

12. Which verses have you memorized most recently?

13. Do you give tithes and offerings regularly?

14. Do you give tithes on your gross or net income? Why?

15. How would you want the finances of your future family to be handled?

16. What is your reaction to the biblical arrangement of the family structure? Why?

17. What are your aspirations concerning your future family, should the Lord bless you with one?

18. Do you love children? Would you want to have any? How many and what composition (subject to Divine approval, of course).

19. What to you constitutes love?

20. Which would you prefer: falling in love or gradually growing to love someone? Why?

21. What are you looking for in a possible future partner?

22. What do you believe constitutes a good and satisfying relationship?

23. How much effort do you put into your relationships?

24. How do you handle misunderstandings, miscommunications, disputes with other people?

25. How do you handle anger?

26. What are some of the things you dislike very strongly, strongly, and

just plain find annoying?

27. What would you do if you were told a friend is spreading gossip about you? Why?

28. What is your reaction to parental involvement in a relationship? Why?

29. What do you consider your strengths as an individual?

30. What are you working to improve in your life?
    a: Spiritually   b: Personally

31. Do you love pets? Do you own one? Which kind?

32. Do you fast (for spiritual, not dietary purposes)? Would you want to include fasting as part of your future family's spiritual worship?

33. Do you support (financially/prayerfully) any Christian work apart from your church? (Christian workers, missionaries, evangelists, etc.)

34. Are you baptized in the Holy Spirit and do you speak in tongues?

35. Do you smoke, drink or use any drugs other than medical prescriptions?

36. During what time of the day do you function best?

37. What principal ingredient do you look for in any relationship?

38. When is your birthday?

39. Tell me about your family: birthdays, anniversary dates, occupations, interests, etc.).

40. Describe your relationship with each of your parents.

41. Describe your relationships with your brothers and sisters.

42. How would you describe the relationships in your extended family?

43. What lesson(s) would you say God is currently teaching you?

44. What plans do you have, both short-term and long-term, and what are you doing to accomplish those plans?

Chapter 7. Recognize the Answer

Summary Review Points

1. Does this person meet every important criterion on your prayer list?

2. Do you agree on important Christian doctrines?

3. Has God provided confirmations?

4. Do you feel unconditional acceptance for this person?

5. Has God opened doors for the two of you?

Application Worksheet

Write down your answers to these questions after you have met the person you believe God wants you to marry.

1. Does he or she meet every criterion on your prayer list? Explain.

   _____

   _____

   _____

2. Do you agree on important Christian doctrines? Explain.

   _____

   _____

   _____

3. What confirmations has God provided to indicate that this is the right person for you to marry?

   _____

   _____

   _____

4. Do you feel unconditional love and acceptance for this person? Explain.

   _____

   _____

   _____

5. Have the two of you seen God open doors for you? Explain.

   _____

   _____

   _____

Chapter Eight

Don't Give Up!

"...Forgetting what is behind and straining toward what is ahead, I press on toward the goal to win the prize for which God has called me heavenward in Christ Jesus." **Philippians 3:13b.**

A final note of encouragement for everyone who has read this book, followed its advice, and is still alone and possibly disheartened. You may have identified and overcome the roadblocks in your way, prayed, acted on your prayers, set deadlines, resisted the enemy, maintained an attitude of expectancy, made your confessions--and nothing happened. Maybe you have met someone that you were sure was to be your spouse, only to be rejected or disappointed.

Don't be discouraged. Like David of old, or the above quotation from Paul, continue to encourage yourself in the Lord. Remember that often your darkest hour is just before the dawn. Satan becomes most aggressive when you are close to receiving your blessings.

Months before I met my husband-to-be, I found myself surrounded with admirers. Needless to say, it was an exciting time for someone who had experienced long periods of feeling unwanted and rejected. So much attention all of a sudden, from respectable Christian men, was fabulous.

Because I was expecting God to send my husband at any time, it was easy to believe that one of these men must surely be the one. In each case, when I thought my years of loneliness were over, I was terribly disappointed. It was tempting to slip into depression and self-pity. But I decided that God had not brought me this far only to turn His back. I was determined that He was going to bless me no matter what! I stood on the promises of God. I kept my confession strong. I resisted the impulse to give in to depression.

You will meet setbacks along the way to marriage. Don't listen to those who would advise you to retreat into the safe assumptions we identified in the first chapter of this book. You have not missed God. A temporary setback does not mean that He doesn't hear your prayers, or that He has no plans for you.

At this point you need to reaffirm your beliefs and continue waiting for your spouse. Don't accept counterfeits or compromises; don't fall into sin or settle for less than God's best. Reevaluate your standards and the characteristics and qualities of the spouse you desire. Reaffirm your stand, and don't dwell on negatives. Don't be tempted to waste today's grace of God on past failures. That is exactly what happens when we begin to focus attention on what should have happened yesterday. Keep thinking about what will happen today and tomorrow. For He alone holds the key to the future.

Do not allow yourself to be overcome by fear. Remember the story of Elijah in *1 Kings 19*. He had challenged all the priests of Baal and made a public show of them. He called for and received God's fire from heaven. He predicted that there would be no rain for three years, and it had happened just as he said. Indeed, he had done great exploits and performed mighty victories and miracles, even causing the destruction of 700 priests of Baal. But when King Ahab told Jezebel all that he had done, she threatened to kill Elijah. What did he do? He fled in fear and self-pity from Jezebel, asking the Lord to take his life.

Isn't that sometimes how we feel? We've seen God work great miracles in our lives, but when Satan attacks with his sharp and painful weapons-- fear, rejection, and disappointment, we give up so easily.

God spoke to Elijah through a still, small voice. People sometimes find it hard to believe that God still speaks to us today, but He will speak to you and guide you toward your victory. You have to be willing to listen to his voice over the noisy throngs who will tell you otherwise. Listen to God; listen, listen, listen, because you want to be alert to the point at which He will say, all right, my son or daughter, you've come so far; now hear what I have to tell you.

If you have faith enough to write down your specific prayer request for a marriage partner, you should have faith that God will give you your heart's desire. Be bold, keep standing, no matter how long it takes. As you see friends and acquaintances getting married, don't envy them. Your time is on the way. The secret of answered prayers is consistency and steadfastness.

Stay firm about what you believe. Use discretion, be selective of those with whom you share your dreams and visions. Many people will try to discourage you; bad counsellors are the death of hope. Find friends who can see spiritually to reinforce your godly vision. Hold the vision dear to your heart.

It is also helpful to pray with someone else in your situation who wants to get married, and to stop thinking exclusively about yourself. Despite the widespread tendency to see individual blessings as a sign of spirituality, you must always remember that Christian life is not about individuality, but community. When we put aside the "me first" attitude toward life, and begin to approach the problems of other people with the same compassion and intensity as we do our own, God has a way of turning things around for us. As God counsels us in *Philippians 2:3-4:*

> "Let nothing be done through strife or vainglory; but
> in lowliness of mind let each esteem others better than
> themselves. Look not every man on his own things, but
> every man also on the things of others."

Finally, my prayer for you is found in *Psalm 20:7, 6, and 1-5.*

> "Some trust in chariots and some in horses,
> but we trust in the name of the Lord our God.
>
> Now I know that the Lord saves his anointed;
> he answers from his holy heaven
> with the saving power of his right hand.
>
> May the Lord answer you when you are in distress;
> may the name of the God of Jacob protect you.

May he send you help from the sanctuary
and grant you support from Zion.

May he remember all your sacrifices
and accept your burnt offerings. *Selah*.

May he give you the desire of your heart
and make all your plans succeed.

We will shout for joy when you are victorious
and will lift up our banners
in the name of our God."

Chapter 8. Don't Give Up!

Summary Review Points

1. Expect temporary setbacks along the road to marriage.

2. Don't allow those setbacks to dampen your determination.

3. Stand on the promises of God.

4. Stay firm about what you believe.

How to Find and Marry the Person God Has for You

Reference Summaries

Chapter 1. Take the Critical First Step

1. Develop a personal relationship with the Lord. This is the critical first step for realizing God's will in every area of your life.

2. Understand that marriage is God's will.

3. Pursue marriage as a high priority.

Chapter 2. Identify the Roadblocks to Getting Married

1. Identify the rationalizations many single people adopt to explain why they are not married.

2. Recognize that those rationalizations or false assumptions are not biblical in origin and become hindrances--roadblocks in the way to finding your mate.

3. Avoid the roadblocks and go on to receive your marriage partner.

Chapter 3. Pray Effectively

1. Realize that prayer provides evidence of your trust in God and in His ability to meet your needs.

2. Use prayer as the most powerful tool for getting an answer to your request.

3. Pray for God's wisdom, knowledge and understanding, a spirit of discernment, and spiritual alertness.

4. Be sure your prayers conform to the Word of God and do not violate His principles.

5. Pray in the Spirit.

6. Pray specifically: write down your criteria for a mate.

7. Pray for the Holy Spirit to help you refine your criteria.

8. Bombard heaven with your fervent prayers.

9. Persist until you know your prayers have broken through to God and it is time to do something.

Chapter 4. Act on Your Prayers as God Directs.

1. Focus on the solution. Don't be problem-oriented.

2. Realize that God expects us to participate in the answer to our prayers.

3. Do something that God directs.

4. Write down your action goals.

5. Confess with your mouth that you will soon be married.

Chapter 5. Resist the Devil

1. Recognize that Satan does not want you to marry, and will do all he can to prevent it.

2. Know the truth of God's Word.

3. Have faith in God.

4. Be alert to the snares and devices of the devil.

5. Put on the full armor of God daily.

6. Pray without ceasing for yourself and others.

7. Resist Satan.

8. Get violent with Satan.

9. Use the authority you have over Satan.

Chapter 6. Maintain an Attitude of Expectancy.

1. Understand that the Word of God is a perfect seed.

2. Hold on to the promises of God; your life depends on it.

3. Be assured that God will keep His Word.

4. Be aware of God's seasons.

5. Maintain an open attitude towards God.

Chapter 7. Recognize the Answer When It Comes.

1. Does this person meet the criteria on your prayer list?

2. Do you agree on important Christian doctrines?

3. Has God provided confirmations?

4. Do you feel unconditional acceptance for him or her?

5. Has God opened doors for the two of you?

Chapter 8. Don't Give Up!

1. Expect temporary setbacks along the road to marriage.

2. Don't allow those setbacks to dampen your determination.

3. Stand on the promises of God.

4. Stay firm about what you believe.

132

WRITE TO US!

We hope you have been encouraged by this book.

We believe that you and many of our other readers will soon have testimonies
of salvation or stories to share of how God led you to your spouse.
Please write and tell us about them.

Victoria K. Fuller
Ada Publishers
P.O. Drawer 1928
Wheaton, Maryland 20915-1928

DO A FRIEND A FAVOR

Do you know of ministers, counsellors, church groups or friends
who might be interested in these materials? Please send us their names
and addresses and we will forward ordering information about

How to Find and Marry the Person God Has for You
and
The Believe God for Marriage Prayer Journal.

Name: _____

Address: _____

City/State/Zip: _____

Name: _____

Address: _____

City/State/Zip: _____

Name: _____

Address: _____

City/State/Zip: _____

Name: _____

Address: _____

City/State/Zip: _____

Believe God for Marriage
Prayer Journal

ORDER TODAY!!

The Believe God for Marriage Prayer Journal is carefully designed as a companion piece for this book,

How to Find and Marry the Person God Has for You.

God says in *Habakkuk 2:2 (KJV)*, "Write the vision, and make it plain upon tables, that he may run that readeth it."

The *Believe God for Marriage Prayer Journal* provides space for you to do just that. This journal will become a handy reference, helping you trace God's steps in answering your prayer for a husband or wife. All of the work sheets from *How to Find and Marry the Person God Has for You* appear in the journal, along with generous writing space, to make it easy for you to refer to them and keep a daily record of your quest.

Here's all the information you need!

This prayer journal was designed as a companion piece for an important new book:

How to Find and MARRY the PERSON God Has for You

To order your copy, or for additional copies of the

Believe God for MARRIAGE Prayer Journal:

**Cut out or copy the order blank below.
Fill it out and mail it to us today.**

_____ *YES! Please send me:*

How to Find and MARRY the PERSON God Has For You

 # copies_____ @ $19.95 each

Believe God for MARRIAGE Prayer Journal

 # copies_____ @ $9.95 each

Please add $4 per book for shipping costs.
Maryland residents add (5%) of total for state sales tax.
Canadian orders must be accompanied by a postal money order in U.S. funds.

Make checks payable to: Ada Publishers, Dept. J
                               P.O. Drawer 1928
                               Wheaton, MD 20915-1928

Please allow 30 days for delivery.

Your Name: _____

Address: _____

City/State/Zip: _____